Sold!

Also by Lois Geller:

Response! The Complete Guide to Profitable Direct Marketing

Customers for Keeps: 8 Powerful Strategies to Turn Customers into Friends and Keep Them Forever

Direct Marketing Techniques

OTHER TITLES IN THE CAPITAL IDEAS FOR BUSINESS & PERSONAL DEVELOPMENT SERIES:

THE 10 LENSES: Your Guide to Living & Working in a Multicultural World by Mark A. Williams
BE HEARD THE FIRST TIME: The Woman's Guide to Powerful Speaking by Susan Miller
MANAGER MECHANICS: People Skills for First-time Managers by Eric P. Bloom
MENTAL AGILITY: The Path to Persuasion by Robert L. Jolles
MILLION DOLLAR NETWORKING: The Sure Way to Find, Grow and Keep Your Business by Andrea Nierenberg
THE NEW TALK POWER: The Mind-Body Way to Speak like a Pro by Natalie H. Rogers
NONSTOP NETWORKING: How to Improve Your Life, Luck, and Career by Andrea Nierenberg
NOW WHAT DO I DO? The Woman's Guide to a New Career by Jan Cannon
THE POWER OF HANDSHAKING: For Peak Performance Worldwide by Robert E. Brown and Dorothea Johnson
THE SAVVY PART-TIME PROFESSIONAL: How to Land, Create, or Negotiate the Part-Time Job of Your Dreams by Lynn Berger
YOUR IDENTITY ZONES: Who Am I? Who Are You? How Do We Get Along? by Mark A. Williams

Save 25% when you order any of these and other fine Capital titles from our Web site: www.capital-books.com.

Sold!

Direct Marketing for the Real Estate Pro

Lois K. Geller

Capital Ideas for Business & Personal Development Series

CAPITAL
BOOKS, INC.
Sterling, Virginia

Capital Books, Inc.
P.O. Box 605
Herndon, Virginia 20172-0605

ISBN 10: 1-933102-27-6 (alk. paper)
ISBN 13: 978-1-933102-27-6

Library of Congress Cataloging-in-Publication Data
Library of Congress Cataloging-in-Publication Data

Geller, Lois K., 1944-
    Sold! : direct marketing for the real estate pro / Lois K. Geller.
        p. cm. — (Capital ideas for business & personal development series)
    Includes index.
    ISBN 1-933102-27-6 (alk. paper)
    1. Real estate business — Marketing. 2. Direct marketing. 3. Advertising,
Direct-mail. I. Title. II. Series.
    HD1375.G42 2007
    333.3068'8 — dc22
                                2006027099

Printed in the United States of America on acid-free paper that meets the American National Standards Institute Z39-48 Standard.

    First Edition

    10 9 8 7 6 5 4 3 2

DEDICATION

This book is dedicated to my mom, Regina Kaufman. She has been an inspiration to me throughout my life. In fact, years ago she sent me a pink spiral notebook and said on the outside: "Isn't it time for you to write a new book?"

Well, Mom . . . here's a new book, one that will hopefully help real estate agents get more business and build relationships with their customers and prospects. Hopefully they will prosper.

I have prospered in life, from all the lessons you taught me, and the love you've given me. Last night I spent with you at North Shore Hospital . . . and now I am in my office sending my chapters to my dear publisher, Kathleen Hughes.

I figure this book is a godsend, because it is keeping me busy, Mom, as I'm losing you.

CONTENTS

Preface   ix
Foreword by Don Peppers and Martha Rogers, PhD   xi

Chapter 1:   Building Relationships with People —
             Not Prospects   1
Chapter 2:   Why Use Direct Marketing to Build
             Your Business?   9
Chapter 3:   The Big Real Estate Offer and The Little
             DM Offer   27
Chapter 4:   Who Are Your Prime Sellers? Who Are
             Your Prime Buyers?   39
Chapter 5:   The Real Estate Website   53
Chapter 6:   The Gold in Your Database   65
Chapter 7:   Direct Mail Creative   77
Chapter 8:   Real Estate Dircct Response Advertising   97
Chapter 9:   Planning a Campaign   113
Chapter 10: DM Math for Real Estate Agents   123
Chapter 11: The Successful Real Estate Marketer   133
Chapter 12: New Creative Approaches   145

Appendix
   I'd Like to Hear from You   155
   Glossary of Direct Marketing Terms   157
   Resource Directory   163
   About the Author   171
Index   173

PREFACE

Several years ago I was happily living in my home in New York City . . . when my Mom's failing health became a number one priority. I had to move to Florida to help with her care—or drive myself slowly into insanity by flying back and forth to Miami each weekend.

As I decided to move, my wonderful staff at Mason and Geller Direct, headed by Michael J. McCormick, Pepper Huff, and Dwain Jeworski, all collaborated and decided to come with me.

That began a strange odyssey of moving everyone, and our offices, to a new and strange place. We were going from brutal cold to hot weather. Even our animals were going to adapt.

In our search, we were looking for realtors to help us, examining MLS listings on the Internet, and talking to acquaintances in Florida . . . and praying our clients would stay with us from Madison Avenue to somewhere in Florida.

One smart real estate person met Pepper and said that we'd all probably be happy near Hollywood (which was also not far from my mom in Miami Beach), and so began the pilgrimage from urban to suburban, from center of the universe to a center with lots of malls.

New homes for everyone, new offices for us—all whet my appetite for my craft to work in this vertical market. Why, I asked myself into the night, hadn't any of our own proven direct marketing techniques filtered into the real estate world?

I've written books on direct marketing, taught many courses at N.Y.U. on the subject, and many corporate courses, yet never saw a real estate agent appear in any of them. Why is that?

Why are millions of dollars spent on real estate mailings each year, without anyone taking advantage of the knowledge we've gained from all kinds of clients who know how to scientifically get results? We test. Measure response, convert them to sales, and continue building relationships with more and more people.

It is a perfect science for real estate. The light bulb went off in my head and I started outlining the book on paper. Then I called my dearest friend in the world, Andrea Nierenberg, about the idea. She said, "Call my publisher Kathleen Hughes at Capital Books. She's wonderful, and you'll be able to offer your conference audiences the books easily with her in charge."

It was like one of those God winks. As I called Kathleen, she liked the idea, got back to me and was 100 percent behind the book because her daughter knows about real estate and knew the power of this subject would resonate with agents who really spend a lot of money on direct mail campaigns that they really can't track . . . with results.

We started collecting real estate mailings from our own mailboxes, ads that seemed interesting, and then lots of mailings from friends and clients around the country.

Then I asked the experts I know in the direct marketing business (I've owned my own agency for many years) for their help. Michael McCormick worked on the mathematics chapter; Dwain Jeworski helped me with the database chapter; Pepper Huff did many of the creatives we give you as examples, and also designed the jacket of this book. Theresa Grant helped get permissions, print out chapters, and organize the process. So many people helped with the content, and especially all the real estate agents who told me all kinds of stories about their direct mail challenges. I appreciate all the time they spent with me.

So, now we're hoping as this book goes to press that real estate direct marketing might change as a result of our work. That you, the reader, will try some of the strategies in the chapters and develop a great brand for yourself, mail to lists that are current with messages targeted to your best prospects. We hope you'll track response, keep in touch with buyers and sellers, and build good relationships with them—and continue to pass on the real solid principles of direct marketing to everyone in your offices.

With the direct marketing know-how you'll gain from _Sold!_, we expect everyone will sell more homes and apartments. And, have more fun doing it! Good luck.

FOREWORD

by Don Peppers and Martha Rogers, Ph.D.

Demographers tell us that there really are people out there who are so lonely, so isolated from others, or so dysfunctional in social settings that they actually revel in receiving more direct mail. They rush to their mailboxes daily, eager to open every item, because each new solicitation received is one more bit of evidence that they are still alive, that they still count somewhere, and that they are still important to *someone*.

There aren't many people like this, of course. We doubt seriously that anyone reading these words is someone like that. The truth is quite the contrary: Most of us don't wait by the curb for the mailman, eager to validate our own existence by tearing open the next sweepstakes promotion or "buy one get one free" offer. No, the vast majority of us are fed up with having our mailboxes stuffed with irrelevant and pointless offers, mostly from companies we don't do business with now and probably won't ever do business with in the future. Many people (maybe some of you?) have placed wastebaskets close by their front doors for the simple convenience of disposing of these kinds of mailing pieces more quickly. For most of us, our attitude toward direct mail is epitomized by the nickname we all apply to it, regularly: *junk* mail.

Well, guess what? This is also the attitude of the vast majority of your own prospective customers toward the mailing pieces you regularly put into the post to them. Sorry, but they aren't eagerly awaiting your message, any more than you are eagerly awaiting a direct mail piece from the local bank or the neighborhood dry cleaner. At most, they will give your postcard or letter a glance for about three quarters of a second before consigning it to the trash. People don't eagerly await mail advertising any more than they eagerly await television commercials. Probably even less, actually.

And yet, still—*someone* must be building business by using direct mail, because it keeps coming, doesn't it? Surely *someone* must know how to make a direct mail campaign work economically for a business. Who are these people and what are their secrets? What differentiates a winning piece from trashcan fodder? How do you capture more than three quarters of a second of attention once you have gone to the trouble of sending your mailing piece into someone's home?

Perhaps you have actually won a new client or secured a new listing — or perhaps just a couple of promising inquiries — by using direct mail. But how do you know, really, that it was your mailing campaign? How does anyone know? And what did it cost you, ultimately? Was the expense and effort worth it?

These are some of the questions you'll find answers for within the pages of *Sold!*, Lois Geller's very helpful and simple-to-understand primer on direct marketing for the real estate professional. You see, Lois really *does* know how to make direct mail work. She has done it her whole career, for a variety of clients and companies. If she can make direct mail work for an auto insurance company, or for a baby food company, or for a tobacco company selling in Russia — well, she can probably make it work for you, too.

By the time you have finished reading this book you will no longer have any doubt at all: Direct mail *can* work for your business. It *can* create a great deal of value for you. Direct mail is a measurable, precise, competitive science — one that serves equally well as a vehicle for experimentation and learning, or for obtaining business results that can be predicted in advance. Business results from direct mail can be depended on like clockwork. All you have to know is how to operate the clock.

Moreover, the postal mail is still as vital and useful a selling tool as it ever has been. More vital, even, because the rapid adoption of Internet technology has fueled an accelerating need for postal mail executions. Customers order catalogs from Web sites, browse the catalogs, then go back online to order. Postcards are as likely to drive Web traffic as store traffic. Personalized e-mail offers get printed and taken to the bank or the store or the movie theatre. At one point or another, nearly every company that puts up a Web site for the benefit of its customers or prospects must use traditional postal mail to fulfill offers, communicate details, or deliver products.

And in your own business, how many of your customers come in to see you only after they've browsed some of the properties for sale online? Did any of these folks first go online in response to one of your mailings? Wouldn't you like to know how to better coordinate your online presence with your off-line direct mail campaigns, so as to get more leverage from both?

The fact is, it would be hard to describe a business *more* suited to direct mail than today's residential and commercial real estate industry. The mail channel is so versatile, so useful, and so rich in possibilities for making local connections and developing useful relationships with people who live in particular neighborhoods or who own particular types of properties, that the shabby quality of most direct mail coming from real estate brokers today is just inexcusable.

So read this book before your competitors do, and put these principles into practice. It won't take long at all for you to measure the results of your efforts. The few hours you spend with this book, and the few dollars you pay for it, will likely add up to one of the shrewdest and most lucrative business investments you make all year.

Don Peppers and Martha Rogers, Ph.D., are founding partners of Peppers and Rogers Group, a division of Carlson Marketing Worldwide. Their books on customer relationships and one-to-one marketing have sold over a million copies around the world in sixteen languages. Their latest book is Return on Customer: Creating Maximum Value from Your Scarcest Resource *(Doubleday, 2006).*

HOW TO USE THIS BOOK

Whether the real estate market is good in your area . . . or not, this book will help you build relationships with more people than you ever thought possible.

It is a way for you to build a pipeline and keep leads flowing into your business. Years ago, Howard Ruff, one of the first financial self-help authors, wrote, "It wasn't raining when Noah built the ark."

So, this book is for you to start building before the rains come down.

This is how it works. Direct marketing is a process. It is not quick, and if you want to do it right and have it really pay off for you . . . it takes some time to learn the process. Once you get it down pat, you will be amazed at the results.

It takes effort to learn this, just like it did for you to discipline yourself to pass your real estate license exam. This direct marketing is a science of getting results. And, I have found from teaching the course in direct marketing at New York University for many years, that it is best to learn it the way you will do it. So, the chapters are in the order that we actually do programs here at my agency for large companies. You might want to skip ahead to "Creative Techniques" (that's the fun stuff), but I urge you to resist that temptation.

Read the chapters in order. Chapter 1, "Building Relationships with People—Not Prospects," tells you why I came to do this book. Chapter 2, "Why Use Direct Marketing Techniques," is next because you might save some money on your general advertising by reading this. You'll also think about issues like who is your best target market (your best prospects). The importance of you (or your company) as a brand is sometimes a new concept for agents . . . and a vital one. Big companies spend millions on brand, and you need to invest something to develop yours, too, because it pays off *always*.

Chapter 3 is the "Real Estate Offer." This is not the offer for the property that you are used to discussing. This is the offer to encourage people to respond to you. It might be an incentive of some kind; and it is way up in front of the book because it is the first reason people have to begin a relationship with you.

Then in Chapter 4 on "Prime Sellers and Buyers," you will learn how your mailing lists are one of the two most important components of your program . . . 40 percent of its success.

In today's world, your credibility is enhanced by your Web site. You need to have one, and Chapter 5 shows you some interesting ones, and layouts you might want to consider for your own.

Chapter 6 is about the gold in your database and how you might want to structure it. Then come the chapters that are the creative ones: Chapter 7 which discusses great direct mail packages (mailings), and Chapter 8 on "Direct Response Advertising" which is how you can begin to get more leads from your advertising by adding a "call to action."

No one likes to plan for anything, but those who do plan always get the best results. So Chapter 9 tells you have to do it. It is not complicated, and you can complete the whole thing on a single page.

Chapter 10 is devoted to how to do the math. How much can you afford to pay for an ad or a direct mail program, and what do you have to get in terms of response and conversion to sales? It is what makes direct marketing a science. You can do a projection ahead of time, then mail, and figure out your own report card. The knowledge you gain will help you so much the next time you go out to do a program.

Chapter 11, "The Successful Marketer," includes some interviews with people I've met in the industry who are successful now . . . and what they are doing. I figure you can get some insider tips from them.

My own dream of doing some breakthrough real estate ads and direct mail are realized in Chapter 12, "New Creative Approaches." I wrote the copy myself and my art director designed them. You can adapt them to your own business — with one request . . . you let me know how they work for you.

Please read "My Final Word." The last page is information about how you can contact me and let me know how your programs are working for you. Please do that, so I can learn from you, too.

So, that's the book in a nutshell. I've included in the chapters my Rules for you to follow, and then some questions for you to fill out at the end of some of the chapters to help you develop the Tools for an ongoing successful career in real estate.

The Rules are from years of experience in direct marketing, and the Tools are there to help you stay on track. The case studies and new ideas

I've come up with for you can be reworked, reinvented, and developed in your own style.

Lois K. Geller
President
Mason & Geller Direct
1400 Marina Drive,
Hollywood, Florida 33019
(646) 723-3231
loisgeller@masongeller.com

Building Relationships with People — Not Prospects

Two years ago, I moved my company from midtown Manhattan to Hollywood, Florida. (Other than the seven hurricanes, it's been great.) In New York, I'd get an occasional mailing from a real estate agent; as a veteran direct marketer, I paid attention to the messages, which were at least direct and to the point.

Real estate agents in South Florida have me almost afraid to open my mailbox. They're sending me scads of strange things to get me to list my apartment or buy a hot property.

Yesterday, for instance, there was this postcard. It came from an agent who wanted to "treat you this Halloween with dependable one-on-one service." Apparently, she doesn't mean it, because the postcard was addressed to Current Resident. And I think she runs a Tex-Mex restaurant, because half the postcard had a recipe for quesadillas. At least I think it was a recipe because most of the words were printed in white type over a photograph of what looked like tacos.

Weird.

They're almost all like that, dozens of them each week—apparently, every real estate agent in four counties wants my business:

> ➤ A photo of a young man and a proud headline "I just sold Apartment 1003 in your building." Well, whoop-de-do.

This postcard with a recipe for quesadillas gave no reason to call the real estate agent.

➤ A grinning couple in matching blazers smiling out at me. Swingers, missionaries, a lounge act, morticians, the ghosts of Ozzie & Harriet?

➤ A generic card with a logo and a photo and some kind of come-on, such as "Sandra Keene, the Condo Queen. Deal with the Best, Forget the Rest."

Houses and condos sell for a lot of money, hundreds of thousands of dollars, millions sometimes. They're worth a little more effort. And the "little more effort" would pay off, big time.

The smart real estate agents I know all build relationships with people, not just prospects. It's wonderful to watch relationships at work.

A client of ours in Moscow, Russia, was ready to retire to Kelowna, British Columbia, and wanted a nice house. I had been to Kelowna exactly once, on business two years earlier, and I'd talked to an insurance agent there. The insurance guy knew a real estate guy and bingo, a million-dollar sale, to a family from Russia! How great is that . . . relationships!

A few years ago, I lived in a coop on East 46th Street in New York, half a block from the United Nations Building. An agent in the building became a friend. His name is Jerry. I learned that Jerry had been doing very well selling apartments in midtown, and he said that his letter campaign was responsible for his success in getting listings.

When I read his letter, I was amazed that anyone had responded. It was long and boring, and it sounded like it was written by a lawyer, which it had been. We reworked it, made it sound like it was from a human being, and response went up 10 percent over the next few months. A 10 percent lift is a lot of money in the real estate business, especially since the rewritten letter didn't cost Jerry a nickel.

Just look at the math over, say, an average year: If Jerry sent out 10,000 letters, got 100 responses and converted 10 of those responses to sales, he did very well. If an average apartment sold for $500,000, and his commission was 6 percent, he made $300,000 from just 10 sales.

After we reworked his letter, he got 110 responses per 10,000 and, though his conversion rate stayed the same at 10 percent, he now made 11 sales and earned $330,000. Not bad.

The next steps were pretty basic:

1. Increase the response rate.
2. Increase the conversion rate.

This is where the magic happens. We won't go into the details of testing here, but we can look at the results. Later in this book, you'll read about testing.

I got Jerry to test different elements of his program, and in the next year his upfront response went from 100 to 105. At the same time, he kept in touch with previous responders who hadn't converted. Suddenly, by testing both his "acquisition" mailings and "relationship" mailings, he managed to lift initial response by 5 percent and overall conversions from 10 percent to just under 13 percent.

The math can get tricky, so here's the short version: Over a year, his 10,000 mailings brought in 105 responses, and 13 percent of them converted to sales. That got him 13 sales a year, 3 more than he was used to. That lift brought in $90,000 more a year in commissions. With a little thought and effort, he gave himself a raise of $7,500 a month!

That kind of success is just the tip of the iceberg. Once a real estate agent understands winning direct mail copy, relationship marketing, response management, testing, offers, lists, databasing, and the magic of small incentives, responses and sales start to spiral up and up.

It's like filling a pipeline with prospects and systematically turning them into sales. At our direct marketing agency, Mason and Geller LLC, we do it all the time with our clients. It just seems that real estate agents haven't quite mastered the science yet. This is a great opportunity for you to do just that.

Even the large real estate companies I interviewed for this book do not understand the science of converting prospects into clients. Many of them show no patience for it, and I think the reason is quite basic: Direct marketing works best in the long term, but every salesperson I've ever met thinks in terms of the next sale.

Short term rather than *long term* seems to be the rule in every business that depends on face-to-face selling, including retail.

That's not a criticism. Personal selling is tough and requires a mindset that operates in the here and now.

Just this morning I interviewed a Maryland real estate agent — a very nice man, who told me how difficult the market is and that everything is slow up there.

I asked him what he was doing about it, and my ears really perked up when he said he was hamstrung. "Real estate is a business of contacts: who you know, how many of them like you, what rung they're on in the echelon of business, and whether they will refer you to hundreds of new prospects," he said, "and I just don't have enough of those contacts."

Every time he mentioned a challenge, I wanted to interrupt with a proven direct marketing solution, but I knew it wouldn't do any good. He sensed, deep down, that developing the right "who-you-know" relationships takes time. But he's stuck in the "sell now" rut. He knows what the solution is, and he knows it instinctively: **relationships!**

That's what direct marketing can do so wonderfully well for you, if you will take the time.

We need the immediate sale, the here-and-now sale, to keep the cash flow up so we can pay the bills. But behind the scenes, step by step, we can build up our long-term program so that six months down the line, the frantic scramble will gradually be replaced with a proven steady flow of quality leads and referrals.

Direct marketing, including the Internet, can help you make contacts, and it's up to you whether they like you. Years ago, the president of Hertz told the head of his ad agency, "Anybody can match any claims we make, any discounts or special services we offer. I don't care about those things; I want people to like us."

It's important that your direct marketing efforts, *all* your efforts, convey your personality. People prefer to do business with people they like. Think of your own day-to-day life: your dry cleaner, favorite coffee shop, restaurant, or bar. There are plenty of these businesses, but I'll bet you spend a lot more at the ones where you actually like the people. Direct marketing works exactly the same way. If people like the personality you project, they will respond. It's human nature.

Direct mail can knock on thousands of doors for you; it can introduce you to the people who live in those homes faster than any one person could ever do in a lifetime. It's both a science and an art. It takes patience and discipline, and you must measure every effort.

The agent in Maryland told me he mails over 10,000 pieces a year, but he had no way of measuring response. He didn't even know you could measure response. You can.

When you don't measure response, you're wasting three things: money, opportunity, and knowledge. *Sold!* is about not wasting any more money on purely tactical communications that almost certainly don't help you get listings, referrals, and sales. This book walks you step by step through the strategic application of proven principles that will build your brand in your market and that will build your own proprietary, predictable selling machine. I'm going to provide you with a systematic approach to being your own direct marketer with DM Rules and Tools™.

Each chapter teaches you how to approach the different elements of your direct marketing program. These are the Rules.

Following the Rules are examples of how to actually implement the Rules — the Tools. You will then add on your own imaginative approach, local color, personality, and information to make the program right for you and your market.

At the end of each chapter, you can answer the questions that will guide you to a successful, relationship-building, direct marketing program, a program that will reap benefits for you by making many new contacts who will be buying or selling properties or referring clients who will.

That's why I'm writing this book. I want you to test reworking your advertising and your direct mail. I want you to make your message more compelling, more interesting, and more relevant to your audience. As you test, you will notice spikes in sales — sometimes small spikes, occasionally off-the-chart spikes. And you will learn something valuable every time out. You will learn how to get people to want you to be their real estate agent . . . and their friends' real estate agent.

You can learn how to do that, step by step, from this book. The outcome will be amazing, because direct marketing, when it's done properly and with patience, cannot fail.

It works for credit cards, catalogs, car companies, insurance companies, publishers, airlines, banks, hotels, and service businesses. It's almost like magic. But it's really just common sense and knowing the ropes. You've got the common sense, and I'll tell you all about the ropes.

Once you get going, I'd love to hear from you. Please write or e-mail me and let me know how you're doing. That's my favorite part of the book-writing business; it's like pulling teeth to get it all down on paper, but it's worth it when I hear from readers. Good luck!

Why Use Direct Marketing to Build Your Business?

I taught direct marketing at New York University for over ten years, and I was delighted to meet so many fascinating people in the class.

They came from all walks of life: dozens of entrepreneurs; salespeople; new immigrants; visitors from the UK, France, Brazil, Italy, Canada, and Turkey; inventors; publishers; ad agency employees; and senior people in large corporations. Some of those executives asked me to teach the course at their companies to improve the skill sets of their employees. The course has taken me to Toronto, Montreal, Moscow, Stockholm, Istanbul, and just about every state in the lower 48.

But my favorite trip was the shortest; just downtown in New York, after a senior manager at American Express invited me to do a two-day seminar for them. I did and got invited back over and over to teach on the 26th floor of Amex's offices in the World Financial Center Tower for many years.

Why would American Express need training in direct marketing (DM), when most of their business is done direct?

That's an easy question for anyone who has ever worked in direct marketing. It's an easy question with a long answer, though. For starters, direct marketing is a humbling business because things change so fast, and if we don't pay attention we'll be out of step in no time. So we always want to learn new things, new trends, new ideas that will propel our direct marketing efforts to new heights.

It's hard to learn new things in a closed environment, especially when the closed environment is a huge company. I'm sure you've heard the old saying that once an organization employs a thousand people, it no longer requires contact with the outside world. Executives and employees often have to step outside to get a fresh perspective.

Then, there's the single focus rut. A list person or database specialist — someone who manages, markets, and rents names to marketing people for direct mail programs — might know everything there is to know about finding the right names for a mailing, but barely have a clue about offer strategy, response management, up-selling, media buying, creative, or any of the dozens of other DM disciplines. So they step outside to learn what they need to know in order to move up in the hierarchy. Step outside or, as in my case, bring in an outsider.

Most often, my inside course at American Express and other companies — which I still offer, by the way — is a refresher course for executives who need reminding about the basics. And the most important basic is this:

> **Direct marketing is a measurable method of selling products and services, generating leads and developing mutually profitable relationships with carefully targeted prospects and good customers.**

It's big business, a very big business indeed. Direct marketing is a three trillion dollar ($3,000,000,000,000) industry, with $145 billion in catalog sales and $50 billion in Web-driven sales. Every time you open your mailbox at home and find an L.L. Bean or Tiffany's catalog, you are part of a direct marketing campaign.

This book is designed to help you begin to build your real estate business by using the techniques I've taught to huge corporations for decades. The principles apply equally to Microsoft and Joe's Software, to Century 21 and Gladys's Real Estate. In fact, the smaller your operation, the bigger your opportunities if you count potential growth.

The Benefits of Direct Marketing

Direct marketers are always talking about benefits, usually as the last element of a triumvirate: features, advantages, and benefits.

The benefits we're talking about are the kind that answer the first question anyone asks when they see an ad, hear or see a commercial, or get a piece of direct mail. The question is this: "What's in this for me?"

Recently, I received a mailing from a real estate agent. It showed a dog, saying, "Let me be your best friend. Thinking of selling your home? Call me today. I'm an expert at fetching buyers."

That's not a horrible approach. It's not good, but it isn't really awful. The basic benefit is that the agent will find lots of buyers. But the reader has to dig for it. The mental process, stream of consciousness, really, goes something like this, with the words moving incredibly quickly through the reader's cerebellum: *"A dog? My best friend? Oh, umm, wait, a dog is a man's best friend. I get it. Is somebody selling me a dog? No, wait, it's about my house. Selling my house? Call me, it says. Call the dog? Call the damned dog? Fetching buyers? The dog will fetch buyers? I don't think so. What is this? Somebody's getting cute with me and . . ."*

The benefit is (a) no big deal, (b) not charming or especially interesting or compelling or memorable, (c) useful only if I'm ready to sell and (d) really hard to understand. It's easy for you and me to understand because we're focusing on it, but our poor prospect is probably standing in the hallway at home with a kid pulling his pant leg, groceries in one hand, briefcase on a strap on his shoulder, and a whole stack of mail he just wants to get through.

The sad truth is that there is no real benefit here.

When direct marketers talk about benefits, we mean strong, clear reasons to respond now. Something like this: "I guarantee that when you are ready to sell your home, I will get you top dollar and I will pay half your moving costs, including packing."

Now that's an offer, but it's really just the attention-getting part of the offer. Now you need details, more reasons for the prospect to respond now, and evidence that you can deliver. Like this, perhaps:

"I've sold 38 homes in the last 8 months and all of my clients were delighted with the results. Here's what three of them had to say, in writing . . ." Then, insert your own excerpts from your testimonials.

"I will show you the original letters and a dozen more when we meet to talk about selling your home. I'll also give you references you can call, and I'll tell you who my banker is in case you want to call him."

"I'll work hard, place ads, call buyers I know, show your home at your convenience, and respect your property. I'll also make recommendations about getting your home to look its best. I'll be working for you."

Make an offer with teeth, credibility.

This answers the *"What's in it for me?"* question. My friend Andrea Nierenberg, the famous networking guru, calls it "everyone's favorite radio station, WII-FM."

The direct marketing offer isn't the kind of offer you're used to. You deal with offers every day, but they're offers to buy. Then there's a counter offer, a little negotiation on the price, a few details like, "Will you leave the chandelier and the drapes?"

Your kind of offer usually comes after someone has seen the merchandise (the house). You've met him or her and now you just have to close. Once the offer has been made, you're halfway there.

The DM kind of offer is nothing like that. For one thing, you're the one making the offer, and you're the one who has to come across when it's accepted. A real estate offer is usually in the hundreds of thousands of dollars. A DM offer almost never involves anything expensive. Ninety-nine percent or more of the people who get your DM offer won't respond at all. Heck, most of them will throw it out before they even know you've made an offer. They are not really prospects. They represent a sort of educated guess about who might be a "maybe, we'll see" pre-prospect.

You just want to talk to them. You have to give them a reason to call and initiate the conversation. You have to give them a WII-FM.

Always remember the WII-FM of Direct Marketing.

You have a very strong "What's in it for me?" If you sell a home, you make a lot of money. It's what you do. You're a real estate agent. You sell homes all the time. Your prospects and clients don't. A lot of them have never sold a home before. Even a frequent mover might sell only once every two or three years. And it is a huge pain in the neck!

Your "maybe, we'll see" pre-prospect doesn't care about you, at least not yet. He doesn't even know you. Your prospect cares about himself. **Everything you say in your direct marketing efforts must be of benefit to your prospect.** You can talk about yourself; of course, you have to, but always in terms of what it means to your prospect.

While you're doing that, think about what you really want your prospect to do in a logical progression. The first thing you want is a response. In fact, that's what you're selling. You want the prospect to get in touch with you to talk about selling (or buying) property. That's all you want. Nothing else is going to happen as a result of your direct marketing efforts. The listing, the offer (your kind), the sale, the closing—all happen later. Nothing happens until you get the response.

Focus on the response. Who's going to respond? Six kinds of people:

1. They've made up their minds and they want to sell.
2. They've sort of thought about it and maybe, well . . . we might want to sell. Let's find out, honey.
3. They've never thought about selling, but, now that you mention it . . .
4. They won't sell in the near future but something about your offer intrigues them, and they're willing to talk, and maybe some day . . .

5. Stop bothering me!
6. A friend gave them the letter you sent and suggested they call you . . .

All six have some potential to contribute to your bottom line. Obviously, you want more of those 1's and if you can get them, great. But everyone else should get some attention, even those pesky 5's, because if you handle them right, they can become 3's or 6's.

We call these six groups *Hots, Warms, Colds* (3 and 4) and *Referrals*. The 5's are called *No's*.

They all have one important thing in common. They have responded to you, and their value to you depends on how you respond to them. Dealing with the people in groups 2, 3, 4, 5, and 6 is where you are really going to shine. If you come across as an agent who's interested only in the immediate sale, they will drop you.

If you come across as the kind of person they want to deal with in the future, a helpful, reliable, stand-up, potentially useful person they want to know, then you will be the agent who eventually sells their home when they're ready. **Direct mail is an inexpensive and very effective way to come across as that kind of person.**

What Is the Difference between Direct Mail and Direct Marketing?

Direct marketing uses all the same media as advertising (TV, radio, newspapers, magazines, even billboards) and a few media that advertising doesn't use very much, including FedEx, UPS, package and billing inserts, FSI's (Free Standing Inserts—you see them in the Sunday newspapers), and so on.

But the biggest medium we use is direct mail, either snail (postal) mail or e-mail. Snail mail is more effective—we'll get into that later.

In any medium, the whole point is to reach a carefully targeted audience with an irresistible offer so they will respond. Choosing the right medium depends on a lot of things, not the least of which is money. See Chapter 10 for information on DM Allowable. Right now, I want to talk more about why DM is so great.

For one thing, there's the D in DM. It means *direct*, between you and your prospect. No middleman (or woman); just you and the people who are going to make it possible to earn scads of money.

DM is advertising, but we never say it that way because that would confuse us with General Advertising, which is really quite different. That's why we call it direct *marketing*. Sometimes we call it direct response. I like that better because it focuses on our goal — *getting a response.*

Whatever you name it, it's profitable, and as you do more of it, it gets more and more profitable because of what you learn as you go along. You learn which media work best, which lists work best, which target audiences contribute the most to your bottom line, which offers work best, when is the best time to communicate, how often to communicate, and much more. That kind of knowledge is worth more than any immediate sales results.

However, you won't learn anything if your DM efforts aren't testable and trackable.

Testing and Tracking

Testing and tracking allow DM to work its magic

Every response that comes in must be trackable to a specific ad, commercial, mailing, e-mail, or internet effort. This allows you to learn the cost of each response, the best offer, the best creative (what we call the pieces in the mailing, ad, or billboard), the most used response channel — phone, mail, online, fax, in person, etc.

I used to say, before I got more polite, that it takes the guts of a burglar to do what we do. Imagine, every aspect of every single thing we do is measured for effectiveness. Not measured in a general way, like "Sales are up this month," or "We had a lot of people at the Open House last Sunday." We're measured in very specific ways, as in "We spent $8,654.32 and six months later we have $42,345.19 cents in profit due to that $8,654.32 investment."

General advertising can't do that. That's not what it does, anyway. It's more about image and brand and quick sound hits. If we both run ads in the same newspaper, and readers notice the general advertising ad, read it, and then turn the page, the advertiser wins. If the reader does the exact same thing to our ad, and doesn't respond, we lose.

Same reaction, but they win and we lose. Weird, isn't it?

They win because every message that gets through adds to the image of the advertiser. We lose because we needed a response, and we didn't get one. Which brings us to a rather stunning conclusion: We aren't really selling what we seem to be selling, whether it's beer, a car, insurance, or real estate. We're selling response! Not just any response, but a qualified response from someone in our target audience.

Direct marketing is all about the number of responses you receive from an ad, direct mail package, radio spot, or television commercial. You can count the number of responses or orders you receive and figure out where they're coming from. You can then use that information to decide how to go forward — by expanding what you're doing, or reworking your plan.

Often in direct marketing, we develop a plan, and in that plan we project the number of responses we think we need based on our Allowable (how much we can afford to spend to get a single response, see Chapter 10) or based on previous tests. So, if last March we mailed 5,000 letters and received a 3 percent response, and this year we think we have a better offer, we might project a 3.5 percent response.

DM lets you grow your customers nationally and internationally

When we started our company, Mason and Geller LLC, we thought our clients would be small or medium sized. It turned out that one of our first clients was a PBS channel in New York, Channel 13; then we managed to get Polygram Music with its 11 different labels, including Mercury, Mercury Nashville, and Deutsche Gramophone. How did we manage to get such large clients? We wrote letters to them. Pure and simple, direct mail letters to the vice presidents of marketing got us in to their offices for meetings, and ultimately they became our clients. So did American Express, California clients such as Code 3 Collectibles, and the *Houston Chronicle* in Texas.

It is amazing how the power of direct marketing can spread your word around the country and to other countries. Roz Ceresne of Keyes Realty told me recently that she places ads in the *Financial Times* around the world and receives calls from many different countries for her properties in beautiful South Florida.

Direct marketing can build your network of friends and help you keep in touch with them for weeks, months, and years

It is always rewarding to have huge networks of people who know about your company and you.

We often forget that people who used to purchase from us and then stopped might be the best potential "new" customers. Why, you ask? The answer is simple: Customers can forget about your company. I purchased magnifier glasses last year at a wonderful website. I bought three pairs. I never heard from that company again.

Last month I was visiting my friend Andrea in New York and she commented on my cute Burberry-looking glasses. When she asked me where I got them, I couldn't remember the name of the website. They should have e-mailed me, sent me a catalog, or kept in touch in some way. Andrea would probably have referred dozens of new customers to the website, because she has more friends than Barney the purple dinosaur, and she gives speeches to thousands of people every month.

"Networking" in the mail has worked wonders for our company over the years. We've published a newsletter called *Inside Stuff.* Every time we mailed it, we would get calls from companies that were interested in having us do a direct mail campaign or improving their websites. It never failed—no matter what the content we used, people called, and business came in as a result.

I'll tell you an inside secret here (if you promise not to tell anyone). There is a way to have even more people respond. When the newsletters were printed, I wrote personal notes on many of those that were going to companies we really wanted as clients. I pointed them to a particular article or asked them how they were doing. The ones that had the personal notes from me often pulled up to a 50 percent response. Therein lays the magic of the personal touch in direct marketing.

Inside Stuff is a free subscription that we offer at speeches or on our website, www.masongeller.com.

Test different offers in direct mail, and keep them secret

If you test a direct mail piece that offers half of your list a free home price evaluation and the other half a free list of suggestions on making their homes more saleable, you can track the responses.

If one is pulling a lot better than the other, you can then roll out to the winner.

How do you track? There are dozens of ways. You might tell the people who were offered the free home price evaluation to call and ask for Peggy Smith (P is for price evaluation), and those who are calling about suggestions for making their home more saleable to ask for Sally (saleable). You then track the calls for each and see which one is pulling better.

It is even easier if you include a direct response card that has postage prepaid. Each card can have a source code on the bottom; for example, P1 (price evaluation, first mailing), and S1 (suggestions for sale, first mailing). Count them, and then you can roll out to the winner. If the price evaluation outpulls the other, you then consider that your control package. This is discussed at the end of Chapter 3 on testing.

If you put an ad in the newspaper, everyone knows what you're offering. In the mail, however, your prospects are the only ones who know what they received. As we consider these more sophisticated tests, real estate agents begin to push back their chairs. Here are some excuses I've heard in talking to them:

- **Direct mail is too expensive to use for the homes and apartments I sell or rent.** "How much is too expensive," I ask? If the answer is "Well, I have no budget," you can't afford to pay for anything. However, direct mail is a targeted piece to someone in your area and it goes right to their home. It will usually work a lot harder to make a sale than anything else you might do.
- **If I received that direct mail piece, I wouldn't respond to it.** Well, if you are a real estate agent, I don't want you to respond to it anyway. You're not in the target audience, have no interest in my promotion, and are not likely to buy a property from me. It is irrelevant that you wouldn't respond.

Many years ago I worked at Meredith Corporation as director of book marketing for cookbooks, craft books, and similar items. At one of our internal meetings, I was presenting an idea for a recipe card collection, and the feature card was for strawberry shortcake.

It showed a luscious piece on the front and the recipe on the back. One of the gentlemen from the accounting department raised his hand and said that he wouldn't respond to that piece, as no one likes strawberry shortcake, and I would be better off showing chocolate cake instead.

Though I valued his judgment in the bookkeeping world, in this case his remarks were irrelevant. First, we were targeting women aged 25 to 45 who were stay-at-home moms. Second, we wanted women who had purchased cookbooks from us in the past. Last, I'd already tested chocolate cake against the strawberry shortcake, and the shortcake out-pulled the chocolate cake two to one.

Although I urge you to show your direct mail piece to many people to get their input, if they are not in your target market and have no concrete reasons for not liking it or why it won't work . . . just disregard what they tell you.

- **My advertisement in the local papers and in the Yellow Pages does fine for me, so I don't need to try direct mail.** This one makes me laugh, as so many real estate agents that I've spoken with have made this remark. My next question to them was, "How many responses do you get from your ads?" They have no idea.

    If they have no idea, how do they know the ads are doing fine? The short answer is they don't. There is no way to track those ads, unless someone calls and says they saw your ad in the *Long Beach Times News* and decided to call. That rarely happens. If there is a receptionist answering the phones, he or she doesn't have time to query clients about where they got the name of the agency.

    In direct mail, if you suggest to the readers that they drop into your agency and bring this certificate, you'll give them a gift book, the *Best Ways to Prepare Your House for Sale*, then you'll know how many leads and clients you received from that piece.

- **I mailed out postcards last year, and they didn't work for me.** This statement goes back to the concept of testing once more. If you didn't mail to the right audience, then maybe it didn't work. Maybe it was not an enticing offer, so it didn't get a good response. Or maybe the tracking wasn't good, so when people called your office, you didn't realize they came as a result of that postcard mailing. Maybe the postcard was not a good vehicle for the mailing. Maybe a letter would have done a lot better.

Based on just one mailing, it is hard to tell. The important thing to remember is that direct marketing is for people who don't get "scared off" when something doesn't work right away. I once told a client that it is for "thick-skinned" people, and sure enough he did last through initial testing and ended up very successful with a collectibles business through the mail.

The one aspect of this that challenges me the most is that people say it "didn't work." Do those same people know if any of their advertising is working? Probably not.

> **Direct marketing works best, when it is a relationship-building, ongoing communication that is relevant to your prospects and clients.**

One way you might consider making it relevant to your target market is to begin with a survey to find out something about the group. That way you can write to them again from a "knowledge level"—based on something you already know about them.

So, if they filled out a survey and said they might be interested in buying a new home in the next six months, you might respond by saying: "You mentioned you might be buying a new home in six months; do you want me to send you a newsletter I've written about the state of real estate in the next year?"

When they respond "Yes," you send them the newsletter with your thanks for filling out the survey. You include another response device in the newsletter, and hopefully a relationship is beginning to form.

You can then always call and check to see if you can help them with suggestions for selling, evaluating the property, and so on.

> **Consider your brand to make yourself memorable to your prospects.**

Your brand strategy will help you to develop all of your tactical programs. That strategy will give you the core of every program and generate the value that will encourage people to want to have a relationship with you. This is a good time to consider the brand. What unique service do you provide that makes you stand out from your competition? How can you best express that to your target audience?

Branding is really your willingness to stand out from the crowd, to do something really different.

In considering your brand and how you're different from all the other real estate agents in your area, ask yourself:

- Is my service *really* unique?
- Do I sell more properties than any other agency? Do I sell them faster? Are my open houses more productive?
- Do I do a better job of marketing my properties with virtual tours on the MLS listings, advertising, and direct mail?
- Do I know the city better than any other realtor? Do I know the schools and find the benefits for prospects who are moving into the area?
- Am I well connected in local groups so that I can help the new family get started with the people they need — pediatricians, clubs, contractors?
- Do I have an interesting story to tell? A hobby that makes me memorable? Am I a star at some sport? Do I have a huge family? What is interesting about me that I can talk about in direct mail that will make people remember me?

Tools

Surveys and questionnaires are tools to get people involved with you. I am including them at the end of some of the chapters of this book, so you can see how you're learning, check your progress, and proceed to do a great direct marketing campaign.

So start now!

Collect some ads from other real estate agents. What do you like about them, what does not appeal to you?

_____

_____

_____

_____

Look at your mail each day and save the mailing pieces you like the most. What makes them stand out for you? Is it the offer? Is it relevant to you? What does it look like?

_____

_____

_____

_____

What kind of a brand personality do you want to convey? Is it down-to-earth, coolly professional, or quirky? Do you want to sound like the familiar next door neighbor, or the town mayor? Write down your idea now, while it is fresh in your mind.

_____

_____

_____

_____

_____

Think about your target customers for a minute. Are they couples with children, young or older? What is their income level? Are they professionals? Are they currently homeowners or renters? Base your ideas on your previous sales history.

_____

_____

_____

_____

When thinking about your previous customers, what are the three things they liked most about you? You can use this in copy later on.

_____

_____

_____

_____

If you were to survey these customers, what would you ask them?

_____

_____

_____

_____

If you have used direct marketing in the past, what would you do differently now?

_____

_____

_____

_____

Take a fresh look at your advertising. How might you improve it? Write down some thoughts.

_____

_____

_____

_____

Remember the offer—have you used one? If not, what kind of an offer could you try?

_____

_____

_____

_____

_____

The Big Real Estate Offer and
The Little DM Offer

An offer in real estate is an opening bid on a property that could lead to a lot of money changing hands. A direct marketing (DM) offer isn't nearly that weighty, but it's deceptively powerful; we'll look at why in a minute. First, let's answer this question: What is it?

A real estate agent making a DM offer is essentially describing, in glowing terms, everything he or she will do for a prospect who becomes a client—plus something extra, what people in New Orleans call *lagniappe* (lan-yap.)

> **Lagniappe:** noun: a small gift, especially one given by a merchant to a customer.

A simple example of a DM offer you've seen many times involves a subscription to a magazine like *Sports Illustrated*. You pay about half the newsstand price, get the magazine in the mail and *Sports Illustrated* gives you something for FREE!!! Like a football phone.

In real estate, your offer would be the sum of your services, your fees (commissions), and the *lagniappe*. The package you offer qualified prospects might look like this:

Free appraisal
Guaranteed bottom price
No hassles, no pressure, ever

(continued on next page)

This website shows that Mr. Smith will do many things to promote my home, so that added value he brings might be why I'd choose him over other real estate agents.

A list of references, including (your) banker
A marketing plan tailored for their property
Recommendations for fixing the property up (staging) to encourage a sale
Help with making those changes
Advertising in print and online
Free online video tour
Extended global network
Open house
Outstanding service
Help finding a new home
Special arrangements for buying a new property
Lagniappe 1: Free packing boxes for the move
Lagniappe 2: Just for responding and agreeing to meet me (you): Dinner for two at a local restaurant. (Good any time in the next month, by the way.)

Some of your offer is business as usual, what we call the "price of admission," and some of it, especially the free packing boxes, is special, above and beyond.

The Something Extra, like *lagniappe* 2, is an incentive that serves as the "call to action." It gets the ball rolling, starts the negotiations.

Why is something inexpensive, like dinner for two at Appleby's, "deceptively powerful?" Compared to a real estate offer to buy, it's almost insignificant.

Well, the offer to buy a property, at best, will lead to one sale. It involves only one prospect. The DM offer could lead to dozens, even hundreds of sales. It will get you on people's radar, it will develop your database, give you valuable knowledge, help you create your own DEW line in the neighborhood. In short, merely by offering something insignificant, you can do yourself a world of good.

DEW line? It stands for *Distant Early Warning*. During the Cold War, it was a bunch of radar stations up by the Arctic Circle that would tell us when Russia had launched missiles in our direction. My father used to say it would give us just enough time to wake Walter Cronkite. Your neighborhood DEW line is all the contacts you make who will let you know the first signs of a neighbor thinking of selling.

So why do you need an offer? Can't you just ask for the listing and include your business card so they'll call?

Well, for starters, there are a lot of agents out there, and almost all of them are doing exactly the same thing. You want to stand out. You want to be seen as professional, serious, approachable, and helpful. You want to demonstrate your *bona fides* with something concrete.

You want people to take action now. Call you. Meet you. Talk to you about buying and selling real estate. Many of them will do that because you laid everything out for them and added something extra. You need your offer to make that happen.

What kinds of offers will interest your prospects? Think *CCI*.

- ❖ Creative
- ❖ Credible
- ❖ Involving

Creative means it's unusual, not the same old thing. (We have an expression for that. It's called MEGO: My Eyes Glaze Over.) It is a good idea to study the offers you get in your mailbox every day and the ads you hear on radio and see in the magazines and on television. Consider the ones you really like and ask people in your target market which ones appeal to them. It's amazing what people will tell you if you just ask. A creative offer can really build your response rate, but, like most of the components of direct marketing, it will work for a while and then stop. You have to test offers all the time.

Offers can get tired when your target audience gets used to seeing them. That happened to me with a catalog I loved. For years, I ordered hosiery from this catalog and each time they sent their "gift with purchase," which was a key chain into which I could insert a favorite photo. After a while those key chains started adding up, and I had dozens of them. So, I brought them to my office and placed them in a large brandy snifter for all to see. I called it the "tired offer display".

I mentioned this when I was speaking at a conference last year and within a week another hosiery catalog landed, unsolicited, in my mailbox. It almost certainly came from a smart marketer who had heard me at the conference. I decided to give them a try — more catalogs arrived, of course, and the Free Gift!!! changed every now and then, plus they sent me a "surprise and delight" *lagniappe* periodically. I still buy from them.

In direct marketing, we follow a rule called the 40-40-20 Rule: 40 percent of the success of your program is the offer, 40 percent is the list, and 20 percent is the creative. Even though offers represent 40 percent of the success of a direct mail program, many marketers send out mail or create a great ad but don't include an offer of any kind, or, even worse, an offer anyone could get even if they hadn't received the mailing.

> For instance, one of my favorite department stores sent me a catalog . . . and yet the offer wasn't credible.

The store is on Fifth Avenue in New York, and the offer was 15 percent off any single product in the catalog. I saw a lovely bowl I could give a friend, so I filled out the order form and sent it in. The next day I was walking on the block where that wonderful store was. I wandered in and was appalled to see a huge *15 percent off everything!* sign hanging from the ceiling.

What's wrong with that? They got my order anyway, didn't they? Well, yes, they did, but next time they won't. An offer in the mail must be unavailable any other way.

Your prospect will respond if the offer is *involving*. Your offer is designed to incentivize people to respond to you for a specific reason (say, a meeting) and then later to list their property with you, send you a referral, buy a property from you, and/or be an ongoing advocate for your real estate business.

❖ Your offer has to be unique (or at least the combination of all the elements of your offer has to be unique.)

❖ Some part of it must appear to give **significant value**. For example, you can arrange to have a designer walk through the house and make suggestions on how it could be made more appealing. The usual offer is an evaluation of the home. That's the norm, almost MEGO, so why not do something better?

❖ Your offer has to be **believable**. That means to pass the sniff test. If something doesn't smell right, people won't respond. For instance, if you offer a FREE stereo system just for responding, people won't believe it. If you enter them in a drawing for a free stereo system, they will believe it. If you tell them you'll buy them a stereo for their *new* home (value $600), they'll believe that and feel they're getting something back from the commission you earned.

The "guts" of an offer can fit into any of several categories:

❖ **Discount:** List your home with us by April 10, and we'll take X percent off our commission

❖ **Multiple Discount:** List your home with us, and we'll cut our commission in half if you purchase your new home through our company network or brokers. Dwain, my company's general manager, made this deal when he sold his home in Connecticut and bought his new one in Florida. Everyone benefited.

❖ **Premium:** Something for free (or a really low price) with the purchase of a product or service. A premium works best when it is related to the product you're selling. So if you're working on getting new listings, maybe a free information book on "How to Sell Your Home Quickly" is one idea to consider. Or, you might consider a hard product, like a free radio or other small gift for responses to your mailing. You can find ideas for all kinds of inexpensive (but very cool) gifts in publications like *Incentives Magazine, Premiums Magazine, Potentials in Marketing, DM News,* and *Direct Magazine.*

❖ **Early Bird:** This kind of offer gets people to act immediately. You might try something like this: The first 10 people at an open house will each receive a Capodimente cup or other small gift. Then you can give each person a number as they arrive to ensure they get their gift as they leave.

❖ **Customer Retention Programs:** You might not think you
want to keep customers for a long time. Who wants to keep
showing properties to the same person forever? But consider the difference one person, the right kind of person, can
make to your business. About seven years ago, I was working with a small agency in Canada on a Canadian Pacific
Catalog. It turned out that one of the partners was very helpful, so we started working with him on other projects. After
three years or so of telecommuting I invited Dwain to work
for us in our New York office. He came down a few times to
look for a house, but couldn't find anything suitable in his
price range. When his Calgary house went to contract, he got
desperate, went online late at night, and found ReMax's Bob
Mori at www.teammori.com, who said he had just the place.
And he did. When we moved our company to Florida, Bob
Mori sold Dwain's house in Connecticut and found the
agent who found the perfect place in the Sunshine State.
Along the way, Dwain has referred friends and neighbors to
Bob Mori. Customer retention (relationship) strategies are
important. The more people you have in your network, the
more leads and sales and referrals you'll get.

❖ **Member-Get-a-Member:** This idea comes from book clubs.
When members refer new members, they get a free book or
some other gift. In real estate, it is a referral. Face to face, you
can get many referrals. If you use the mail, you might be able
to get a lot more, especially from people you've helped in the
past. All you have to do is ask and reward. I know an agent
in New York City who gets all his business this way, and he's
very wealthy now. Direct mail lets you ask for referrals from
people you don't even know.

MCI, before they partnered with Verizon, became very well
known because of their *Friends and Family* program. Customers got
discounts for referring other customers PLUS a lower per-minute
rate when they called other MCI customers. At the time, it was a
very big deal.

Your own referral plan can be a reward system. You can give
cash, gifts, gift certificates, savings bonds for kids' education, or
any creative idea you have. If people in your neighborhood are

already calling on people (like an Avon or Tupperware rep), they might be able to help you get referrals; in that case, you might offer them part of your commission on each sale.

You can even make it a game for everyone in your referral network. My friend, Marla Altberg, president of Ventura Associates, which provides "off the shelf" sweepstakes for companies to cost-share, sent me this story about a mortgage company she's working with:

> *A client of ours, a major national bank and mortgage company, purchased the mortgage portfolio of another bank. As a result, all of the mortgages of the acquired bank were now re-named as mortgages of the new bank. To allay fears of the mortgage holders and promote goodwill, the new bank conducted a sweepstakes. It was delivered in the mortgage statements as a direct mail statement stuffer, with a secondary objective being that of e-mail (address) collection. These e-mails would facilitate future low-cost communication with the customer database.*
>
> *This sweepstakes promotion featured a two-pronged approach. First, we offered prizes that we knew these consumers wanted to win – specifically a year's free mortgage payments as the grand prize, or a month's free mortgage payment as secondary prizes. What better incentive could there be to reward potential loyalty! In addition, we utilized the programmed learning technique to educate consumers on the benefits of the new bank, incorporating humor as a fun involvement device for increased knowledge retention.*
>
> *It was executed quite simply with a three-panel brochure, giving a brief story of how the bank was founded in the stagecoach days of the Wild West. Participants were then asked to complete a brief multiple choice quiz to qualify for sweepstakes entry. Many of the answers were funny, but still reinforced the service and reliability aspect of the bank's mortgages. The result was a blockbuster response rate of nearly 25 percent, with approximately one-third of the participants supplying their e-mail addresses. It was so successful that the client repeated the promotion.*

In direct marketing, we TEST offers. Remember the 40-40-20 Rule: 40 percent Offer, 40 percent List, and 20 percent Creative. Test the offers against each other and see which one wins. The winner becomes the control, and then you test new offers against it. Remember to analyze test results and watch your business grow quickly.

Testing is an integral part of direct marketing, even if you have a small budget. How will you know which offer is working best for you? Which would draw a better response: a discounted commission or a free evaluation? A premium or a sweepstakes? The best way to find out would be to take a poll—ask each of your clients and potential clients which offer would make them want to work with you. Since that's not a very efficient method of gathering this information, your alternative is to try one offer, try another, and try yet another until you find the one that works best for you. Even better, test all offers at the same time.

When large companies test, they use charts and probability tables to track the return percentage of each offer. However, even real estate offices with limited mailing lists and databases can make testing simpler and more efficient by following these procedures:

☞ *Test only one feature at a time.* In other words, you can change the offer, and you can change the package, but not at the same time. If you were to change more than one element, you wouldn't know which change buyers were responding to. Test an offer of a free staging against a free marketing plan, for example.

☞ *Code your tests so you can measure results.* Each version of a promotion must have its own code so that you will know exactly which ones garner the best responses. Suppose you run the same direct response ad in two different magazines. For testing purposes, the only difference should be the code printed on the coupon, so that when you receive the orders you'll know which magazine delivered more buyers. You can also do this by having one ad say, "Ask for Patty" and another say, "Ask for Connie."

☞ *Keep accurate records.* Coding doesn't mean anything if you don't keep track of the results. In the example above, if you receive 50 responses from Magazine A and 18 from Magazine B (assuming they both cost the same and have similar circulation), you would obviously choose to continue advertising in Magazine A. If one offer draws twice as many responses as the other, you'll want to discontinue the less effective one. Whether you tally responses in a computerized database or write them in a ledger book, be sure to keep an accurate count of which tests produced the best results.

☞ ***Analyze test results and take action.*** When the testing is completed, ask yourself this simple question: "What did I learn from this test?" If you have kept accurate records, your test results should clearly indicate the actions you need to take to capitalize on those results. If your reduced commission is producing the greatest responses, that is the offer that should be repeated.

Summary

People respond best when there's a unique offer that's creative, compelling, involving, and believable. Even the best offer gets tired, so keep testing new ideas. One great way to find new offers is to watch what you get in your own mailbox and adapt those ideas to your own business. Also, you want all your hard work to count, so remember always to test and track—and try, try, try again.

Two-Step Direct Mail Program*

Test	Offer	Response
Seminar Test	Free mini-seminar on how to fix up a "doghouse" and turn it into a "dollhouse."	60 Showed up 20 Leads 2 Conversions to buy/sell
Relocation Packet Test	Send/ Offer a free Relocation Packet. It includes an introduction to a vast	200 Requests 60 Leads

	array of community information, including area schools, parks, recreational activities, youth sports, housing, business climate, and current events.	5 Conversions to buy/sell
Home Value Analysis Test	Free home value analysis. Included are details on homes that have sold in your area within the last 12 months. Filled with charts and graphs.	90 Requests 35 Leads 2 Conversions to buy/sell
Home Inspection Test	Free professional home inspection. Inspector is certified by the Home Improvement Commission and accepted as an expert witness by administrative law judges in cases heard before them.	300 Requests 60 Leads 20 Conversions to buy/sell

*This is not an actual Offer Test chart

Here are **the Rules:**

- People will respond if you have an offer for them.
- "Free" is a great offer if it is believable. But sometimes asking people to pay for something qualifies them better as prospects. This came from a Dear Abby column in 2006:

Years ago, our local chamber of commerce sent 10 underprivileged kids to two weeks of overnight camp. Five of them paid $5.00 and five paid nothing. Upon their return, we received five thank-you notes from the ones who paid. We heard nothing from those who attended for free. I think people only put a value on things that cost them something.

- Make your offer creative. If agents in your area are offering a free home evaluation, you go them one better.
- Test one feature at a time.
- Code your tests.
- Keep accurate, up-to-date records.

Here are **The Tools:**

Is your offer creative and different from others in your market?

_____

_____

_____

Does your offer involve your prospects, like with a contest or survey or sweepstakes?

_____

_____

_____

Is the offer believable? Does it pass the sniff test?

_____

_____

_____

It is always best to test more than one offer at the same time. What ideas do you have for offers right now, and how will you code them so you can track response?

_____

_____

_____

You have to measure your results, so remember to ask prospects how they heard about you. Keep accurate records. It helps to have a tracking sheet ready ahead of time.

Who Are Your Prime Sellers? Who Are Your Prime Buyers?

Your goal is to get the right offer *into the right hands* at the right time. The most brilliant creative with the most compelling offer won't do you much good if it doesn't get to the right people.

Harley Davidson doesn't write to many octogenarians (wrong hands.) Nor do they offer test drives in January in International Falls, Minnesota. (Wrong offer, wrong time.)

In order to get your offer into the "right hands" via the mail, you first have to get a list of the right people; it's up to you to describe, as completely as you can, what kind of people are the right ones for your business. Some direct marketers—I'm one of them—insist that lists are responsible for 40 percent of the success of a direct mail program.

There's a formula we use: Lists 40 percent, Offer 40 percent, and Creative 20 percent. But remember — the wrong lists can be responsible for 100 percent of the failure of a DM program. One of the great mysteries of the universe is why so many mailers spend nearly all their time on creative and so little time on the things that really matter. I suspect that the word "creative" is responsible. Everyone wants to be thought of as creative. The reality is that creative is a bad term for the words and images we use in direct marketing. *Salesmanship in print* is a better term. In fact, I believe that most good salespeople who've never written a thing could write a better direct mail letter than a creative writer who's never sold anything.

Most of the real estate agents I interviewed for this book told me that they put together their creative, develop a few good offer tests, and *then* try to figure out who they should be mailing to. Usually they wind up using whatever lists their printers and lettershops recommend. Some agents just get every homeowner's name and address in a particular ZIP code. This is backwards. Lists come first. Before you do anything, get the whole notion of lists down pat.

Talk to a Smart List Broker

There are hundreds of list brokers in the United States. Nearly all of them belong to the Direct Marketing Association, which you can find at www.the-dma.org.

Don't confuse list brokers with list managers. Although some companies are both, the functions are quite different. List brokers work for their clients, the mailers — you, in this case. List managers work for the owners of the lists they manage.

If you're a very small mailer, you're not going to find many list brokers who want to work with you. Let's say you might mail 50,000 pieces a year, an average of about 4,200 a month. That means you'd spend about $600 a month on lists. Brokers get about 20 percent of that. In this case, that would be $120, which might get you an hour's work.

Most list brokers do a great job coming up with detailed list recommendations as long as their clients tell them what they need.

Before you meet a list broker, you should write down all the attributes of the people you want to reach. And there are a lot more attributes than this obvious one: *People who want to buy or sell a really expensive, easy-to-move property, right now.*

But that's not a bad place to start, because you can think about it this way: *What kind of people* in your market are most likely to want to buy or sell a very nice property within the next six months, year, two years, or three years? I don't know the answer, but I suspect it contains some of the following:

Happy past clients:
- People who've bought from you before
- People who've sold through you before
- People they've referred to you
- People who've talked to you about buying or selling

People you know personally from these potential prospects:
Married
- Just married
- Starting a family

Single women
- Career women
- Separated/divorced women
- Widows

Single men
- Retirees (or soon to be)
- Empty nesters (or soon to be)
- Just promoted to a better paying job
- Just got transferred out of town
- I'm sure you can think of some more.

Your absolutely best list is your own list of past clients, referrals, and inquirers. This should contain more information than just name, address, and phone number. Because you've met these people, you can add everything you know about them including years they've lived in their home, life stage, ages of kids, probable income, vacation home, personal preferences, plus any relevant observations you made while dealing with them. (One of the first things you do with this information is look for things-in-common among the clients who've done you the most good.)

But what about outside lists? I asked Dolores Ryan Babcock, executive vice president of Direct Media, Inc., and one of the smartest people I know in the list brokerage business. When I was teaching the direct marketing course at New York University, Dolores handled the session on lists, and the students thought she was great. She works with catalog companies like Lillian Vernon, Omaha Steaks, and Spiegel to get the right lists for their programs.

Here's what she suggested for real estate agents:

We have been doing this kind of work for seminar companies and dealer groups for years. The key is providing the most up-to-date names and selections for each group at the most efficient cost. The only way to do that is to have the corporation rent the database (with millions of names on it), and provide them to the sales agents and Realtors throughout the country. That way the file can be selected with information on children in the household, ages of the children, number of years at the residence, approximate value of the home, and all kinds of other information the salespeople might need.

Otherwise, you are renting names that may be old and outdated and have little information on the file. And the agent pays a lot of money for that rental. When the corporation rents it, their large-scale cost efficiencies kick in and the individual agent will pay less for a better, smarter list to mail.

Types of Lists

Traditionally in acquisition (finding new customers and prospects), the lists we rent are other people's customer or inquirer files. There are thousands of them available in two broad categories: compiled and direct response lists.

Compiled Lists

An agent in Maryland told me that he rents lists of people who live in subdivisions in his area. That's considered a compiled list. They are derived from telephone books, public records, and car and voter registrations. All of those interests are coupled with the geographic area and particularly the ZIP codes you select.

Generally, the names on compiled lists are people who have one or two things in common: dentists in Manhattan, for example, or real estate agents in southwest Topeka. Business-to-business (b2b) marketers use compiled lists a lot. We worked for The Thomas Register of American Manufacturers for years, and their mailings soliciting advertising generally went out to manufacturers on all kinds of compiled lists.

Compiled lists are less expensive than response lists, and they're fine for reaching all the people in a neighborhood. They give you the quantity of names (what we call *the count*) you want, but they will rarely give you the best possible response. The reason is that people on a compiled file are not proven responders. Another reason is that the lists are often not as up-to-date as they should be.

Direct Response Lists: Proven Responders

A direct response list consists of people who have responded to a DM offer from a company other than yours. (If they responded to your offer, they appear on your own house file.)

Direct response lists generally perform much better than compiled files. For one thing, they're usually up-to-date because they come from the company's house files. The people on the lists have already bought something in response to a direct marketing effort so they have a higher likelihood of responding to other offers. Since you're going to be mailing to those people, you should look on the list cards to see how many of the names are "direct mail sold," which means they responded to a direct mail effort. Now, of course you don't expect anyone to buy a home or apartment in the mail, but you do want them to respond to your offer so you can begin a relationship with them; in the future they might buy or sell a property or refer you to someone who will.

How Do You Choose a List?

Your first choice of a list is your own prospect file, or perhaps the file they provide you in your real estate agency. The next best list, of course, would be your competitors' prospect files, but I doubt they are going to rent you that list.

Then there is the third best list choice, people who have characteristics similar to those of the people on your house file. In other words, you are looking for a list of people who are very similar to the buyers or sellers from your own file.

I asked Henry DiSciullo, Director of Direct Marketing Services at Automated Resources Group International (ARGI), about the ideal list for a real estate broker. Henry is very smart about finding people who have the highest likelihood of buying.

*The key solution is a **database**, incorporating lists that nationwide and local realtors can effectively use for prospecting purposes. The challenge is to populate the database with the right mix of lists targeted to home buyers/sellers and to keep current the information flow into the database.*

The marketing challenge facing Realtors, be it national chain or a local sole proprietor, is that they are local businesses so they need data on a local level. The mass compiled lists are probably not much better than a phone book.

The two challenges a Realtor will face are: (a) finding the list(s) that reach potential "pre-movers" and (b) the minimums associated with renting most lists, usually 5,000 or 10,000 names per list (so, if you want to try four lists, you might need to rent 20,000 names even though you are going to mail just 5,000 at a time. There are ways around this. For example, you might be able to negotiate to use the names you rent over three months.) With this as a backdrop, my suggestions are as follows:

Potential markets that identify a pre-mover are:

- *Pre-Natal lists matched with renters. This group has a higher proportion of movers than the general population.*
- *New Birth lists matched with renters, same as Prenatal.*
- *College Students (Senior Class only).*
- *Home/Property related data.*

Because these lists would probably be too expensive to cover the minimums in a specific geographic location for a single Realtor, some central entity must build a realtor marketing program/database with a web based access/delivery (see www.archtelecom.com/industry/ real_estate.asp).

If there was sufficient financial interest, develop a prospecting database with several unique source feeds of information that would

*allow for analytical segmentation, which Realtors could access via the
Internet. We could have the lists above integrated into a prospecting
database which Realtors could order online. For national Realtors,
(e.g. Coldwell Banker, Century 21, ReMax) agencies could offer a
turnkey program of data, and direct mail for any participating local
real estate agent."*

Step 1: Consider the people you have now

What kind of customers do you have? Are they mostly men, women,
or couples? Do most of them have children? What is their age range?
What is their income level?

If you're not sure about this information, you might consider
pulling one or two hundred names of people who have listed
with you, or bought from you, and send them a survey. You
could also do it on the phone. I'd position the survey as a way
you are trying to improve your service. Ask them the questions
you need answered. And, as long as you're talking to them,
invite them to send you a referral if they know of someone interested in buying or selling a home. Make sure you tell them you'll
be sending them a gift card from Barnes and Noble or Macy's or
Home Depot as your way of saying "thank you." (Your survey
might pay for itself, and the gifts would generate word of mouth
advertising.)

Step 2: Consider what your best customer is like

What do your customers have in common, besides the fact that
they are moving from their homes? What kind of vacations do they
take: the Riviera or Disney World? It is a good idea to put a face on
these people, so you can "bridge" to them in your copy.

*You recently took a trip to Disney World, so you are probably the
kind of family that likes to be together in a lovely warm climate. So I
thought I'd write to you about our new vacation development for
families in Miami Beach.*

Since you rented a list of people who had recently vacationed at
Disney, it was an easy bridge for you to offer them your new vacation homes. We call that "working from a knowledge level."

Step 3: Talk to a list broker

A list broker's job is to match up mailers with list owners. You have to give them information on who you want to target, who your best customers usually are, and whether you focus on buyers or sellers.

The broker will then come back to you with recommendations. It is important to choose a list broker wisely. Many agents I've interviewed have told me that they acquire their lists from a printer or lettershop (mailing house). Not a good idea, because you rarely get enough information.

Use a real list broker. You can call your local chapter of the Direct Marketing Association and ask for a few recommendations. Ask each broker for client references, and then inquire about lists you might use.

When you receive the proposals, you will have a good idea which broker will do the most work for you. Ask them why they recommended a particular list and how often that list is updated.

Sometimes list brokers tell you the most amazing results they've had, and you can learn from that. I remember working with a client years ago to sell computers in the mail. My brilliant broker told me that people who bought piano music in the mail might be a good test. I'm not sure to this day why that list of piano music buyers pulled such a high response for an expensive computer, but it did.

Step 4: The list broker sends you a list plan with list cards

A list card tells you the quantity of names on the list, gives you tons of other information and the cost per thousand (CPM.) Typically the base cost of a list is $75 to $125 per thousand names you rent. You'll note that I always refer to renting—not buying—the names; you normally do that for one-time use only, unless you make special arrangements.

You'll notice that most lists offer many Selections, and they cost extra, usually something between $5 and $15 more per thousand.

If you don't ask for selections, you'll get a random selection of names from the list. That's not good enough. You might, for example, wind up with names from all over the country when you need names from just a small part of your market.

Selections are important. You may be interested in a particular area of town, one ZIP code, and maybe the sectional center. You might want to select males, at a certain income level in ZIP code 33109. You might also want men who have bought something recently (hotline names). So, you might select a list with a base price of $100 per thousand. Then you want the selection of males ($10 per thousand) who have purchased recently ($20 per thousand.) The ZIP code might add $5 per thousand, bringing the total to $125 per thousand for the names you want to rent.

People who have recently purchased something have a high propensity to purchase again. Now this may or may not be relevant in real estate, but it is worth consideration. If someone has recently had a raise, is buying a car, or making another major purchase, they may also be considering buying a second home or moving to a better primary residence.

Description of Buyers, a section of the list card, tells you something about the type of people who purchase from the list owner.

One other thing to watch for: Some list owners won't rent to mailers making soft offers. Those are offers prospects don't have to pay for: a gift for filling out a survey, for instance, or free information. My guess is that you'll be making a lot of soft offers.

Step 5: You choose your list(s)

And on your lists will be the up-to-date names and addresses of people a lot like your current clients. They'll be proven direct mail responders and likely to move soon. When they respond to you, they go onto your database, and you'll develop long term and mutually beneficial relationships with some of them.

Step 6: Your list broker sends the names to your printer or lettershop, usually by email

You never get the names. When you think about it for a minute, you'll realize why. The lettershop or printer then addresses your mailing in whatever way you've asked for and arranges for it to get into the mail stream.

Look at the examples of lists you might want to test. Remember to ask your broker when the list was last updated. The more current the names, the better they'll work for you.

GeoNeighboring Database

Data Verified: Oct 24, 2003.   Mid 332037-000

GeoNeighboring Solutions, Inc.
  4350 Georgetown Square, Suite 701, Atlanta, GA 30338-6219.
   Phone: 888-561-7176. Phone: 770-458-3154. Fax: 770-458-4245.

PERSONNEL
List Mgr—Matthew Nelson

SUMMARY DESCRIPTION
Database that targets the closest 50-500 neighbors around existing customers of contractors, retailers and household service companies, selecting only prospect neighbors that match the demographic profile of these customers within a specific distance (500-5,000 feet), and providing the street names of these customers for use in the mail piece as an implied referral to increase credibility.

LIST SOURCE
Compiled directories, public records, questionnaires, and direct response programs.

SELECTIONS WITH COUNTS
                              Updated: Oct 24, 2003.

	Total Number	Price per/M
Total list	100,000,000	*75.00

  (*) Volume pricing: 5,000-49,000, 75.00/M; 50,000-100,000, 65.00/M; 100,000-199,999, 55.00/M; 200,000 or more, please inquire.
Minimum order 5,000.

OTHER SELECTIONS
Marital status, dwelling type, length of residence, presence of children, estimated HH income, age in 10 year ranges (18-24, 25-34, 35-44, 45-54, 55-64, 65-74, 75+), 5.00/M extra; homeowners, age of structure, 7.50/M extra; direct mail responder/buyer/donor, telephone numbers, 10.00/M extra; adult age specific (MM/YY of birth), 15.00/M extra; telemarketing prospect report, 25.00/M extra.

COMMISSION, CREDIT POLICY
30% commission to brokers.

METHOD OF ADDRESSING
Mag tape, 25.00 fee; electronic transfer, 25.00 fee; telemarketing prospect report, 25.00 fee; CD-ROM, 50.00 fee.

DELIVERY SCHEDULE
Delivery from 5 to 10 working days.

RESTRICTIONS
One time use only. Repeat usage by special arrangement.

UPDATE SCHEDULE
Updated quarterly. NCOA. CASS certified.

A mailing list data card that is currently available for real estate agents.

Homeowners By Home Value

Data Verified: Jan 5, 2005.

Mid 630349-000

Homeowners Marketing Services, Inc.
12444 Victory Blvd., 2nd Floor, No. Hollywood, CA 91606.
Toll Free: 800-232-2134. Fax: 818-505-9729.
E-mail: bj@homeown.org

PERSONNEL
List Mgr—Bernie Josephson
E-mail: bj@homeown.org

SUMMARY DESCRIPTION
Individuals who have purchased a home, townhouse or condo with home value.

LIST SOURCE
Compiled New county court registration records of grant and warranty deeds.

SELECTIONS WITH COUNTS

Updated: May 28, 2004.
Counts Thru: Dec 2004.

	Total Number	Price per/M
Total list	15,236,636	65.00
Home value:		
$60,000-$79,999	406,507	65.00
$80,000-$99,999	230,764	65.00
$100,000-$124,999	221,897	65.00
$125,000-$149,999	231,685	65.00
$150,000-$199,999	192,654	65.00
$200,000-$249,999	213,834	65.00
$250,000-$299,999	97,686	65.00
$300,000-$399,999	50,733	65.00
$400,000-$499,999	43,296	65.00
$500,000-$999,999	16,212	65.00
1,000,000+	24,066	65.00

No Minimum: $75 computer fee on orders under 15,000 names.

OTHER SELECTIONS
State, Zip, code line, county, mortgage amount, ethnic, income, loan type, loan to value, key coding; gender, marital status, down payment select, nth select, equity, presorting, 5.00/M extra;

This list data card includes the current home value, so they may be targeted with the right property.

Homeowners By Length Of Ownership

Data Verified: Jan 5, 2005.   Mid 630360-000

Homeowners Marketing Services, Inc.
  12444 Victory Blvd., 2nd Floor, No. Hollywood, CA 91606.
  Toll Free: 800-232-2134. Fax: 818-505-9729.
  E-mail: bj@homeown.org

PERSONNEL
List Mgr—Bernie Josephson
  E-mail: bj@homeown.org

SUMMARY DESCRIPTION
Individuals who have purchased a home, townhouse or condo and still live there.

LIST SOURCE
Compiled New county registration records of grant and warranty deeds.

SELECTIONS WITH COUNTS
                        Updated: May 28, 2004.
                        Counts Thru: Dec 2004.

	Total Number	Price per/M
Total list	12,804,463	65.00
1978-1983	729,400	65.00
1984-1988	1,720,544	65.00
1989-1993	3,309,919	65.00
1994-1998	7,044,630	65.00

No minimum: Computer fee of $75 on orders under 15,000 names.

OTHER SELECTIONS
State, SIC, key coding, county, home value, mortgage amount, ethnic, income, loan type, loan to

This list might be used for people who have been in the same home for four years or more in one or more ZIP codes.

TOOLS for working with lists

First, consider what your current clients have in common. What are the attributes of your best clients? Are most of your clients buyers or sellers? Also, take a look at your past clients and prospects to see what they might have in common with your current clients.

_____

_____

_____

_____

_____

_____

Unsure about your clients' demographics? Consider putting together a short survey . . . in order to improve your service. Here are some things to think about when considering a survey: Make it personal, use your voice (remember, it's you talking to your clients). Invite them to refer someone who is in the market to buy or sell. Always remember to thank them and offer them a gift for responding.

_____

_____

_____

_____

_____

Ask for a list plan from a new broker. What did he give you that looks promising?

_____

_____

_____

_____

_____

The Real Estate Website

For years my computer was basically a typewriter. (For younger folks, a typewriter is . . . *a writing machine that produces characters similar to typeset print by means of a manually operated keyboard that actuates a set of raised types, which strike the paper through an inked ribbon.*)

Then along came the Internet and e-mail, then pictures, e-commerce, and, *ta da*, we could shop without leaving home.

As you know, people now shop online for new homes without leaving their old homes and most real estate companies are getting pretty good at using the Internet to present properties. It saves everyone a lot of time and energy. But it isn't easy.

When the Internet first came along, marketers leaped on the idea because it offered the potential for unlimited "reach" at very low cost. In theory, you could spend a few thousand dollars on a website and everyone with a computer could access your site, view your properties, gather information, and sales would boom. Marketing nirvana.

It hasn't worked out quite that way. The first problem is that every dog and his uncle put up a website. There are now gazillions of them. Google *south Florida properties* and you'll get 126,000,000 results or about 15 times as many hits as there are people in South Florida; *south Florida real estate* and *south Florida homes* each generate about 120,000,000 hits. This is insane.

The promise of unlimited reach at extremely low cost resulted in exactly what an economist would have predicted: swarming, exactly as if you were offering free money.

Soooooo, what do you do? How do you get Internet searchers to visit your website? With millions and millions of options, why should they pick yours?

The answer for the big companies with staffs of Internet and computer experts is something called *web optimization*, a complicated and expensive program involving the latest software constantly updated, meta tags, key words, working with search engines and "net directories," reciprocal links arrangements with other companies, daily refreshing of content, online ads, and paying for position (getting as close as possible to the top of the first page of a search result.)

To most of us, though, developing and maintaining a useful website is a persistent challenge. In the early 1990s, Mason & Geller set up our first "website" — in quotes here because our first effort was just a static Web page with basic information.

Then, we began to add content: my columns on creative, PowerPoint slides from speeches and seminars, a list of our preferred suppliers, ideas, samples of our work; then information about our Direct Marketing Boot Camp (seminars we offer to corporations all over the world); and some of my books. We have a newsletter you can subscribe to free at www.masongeller.com, and we run goofy contests every now and then. (*Clean Lois's Credenza!*)

Over the years, our website has morphed into an important relationship marketing tool for our company.

The Internet Is Even More Important for Your Business

In *The Realtor® Magazine* (Leadership Issue 2006), Mark Weithorn, President of Digital Printers International, wrote

"Imagine talking to a client who is across town or across the country. You are telling them about a property. You say: 'Are you next to a computer? Please go to my website.' You are both then able to look at the same pictures and details for a particular property. The bottom line is that if you don't have a presence on the Internet, you are working too hard and missing a ton of leads. A website also tells people you are a true professional, a businessperson." Mr. Weithorn added some eye-opening statistics:

- *Eighty-five percent of all homebuyers and sellers do research on the Internet before calling a Realtor.*
- *Ninety percent of these people use a Realtor*
- *Seventy-five percent of these people use the first Realtor they speak to.*

But before any of that can happen, you need to get people to your website

There are many ways to do that, but the first step is to print your web address (URL) on everything: business cards, letterhead, ads, direct mail pieces, yellow pages. Mention it during speeches and radio interviews, to friends, prospects, and so on. Some Realtors print their URLs on refrigerator magnets and on giveaways like pens and calculators.

Search Engines can help you get prospects from anywhere in the world

You use search engines every day; some of them aren't really search engines, they're directories, but that doesn't really matter to us. The most popular search engine is Google, but MSN, Yahoo, Ask, and 157 others all get used by millions of people. Getting your website near the top of a search result requires time and expertise that you and I don't have, but there are plenty of companies that can help you if you really want to follow that route. My instinct tells me that if you work for a big company, the search engine issue is under control, and if you're a small company you can't afford to get to the top of the list and will have to rely on other ideas.

The other ideas involve what I call the Internet Paradox

To psychologists, *Internet Paradox* means that we're all linked online now, but we spend so much time alone in front of the computer that we're all farther apart. My notion of Internet paradox is that you need to use another medium to drive traffic to your website.

You can, and probably should, advertise your website with small ads in local weeklies, the yellow pages, billboards, supermarket take-ones, postcard mailings, event marketing, and so on. All inexpensive. Remember that you are advertising your website, so you need one strong, consistent element — your name and your URL. Nothing else. Everything else you want to say and show can be on your site.

Make your homepage user-friendly (clear and easy)

Too many real estate agents try to make their websites overly fancy with tons of graphics, funky fonts, and too much copy, especially bad when it runs over photos, all of which just irritates the average visitor. It's important to remember that your prospects might see dozens, even hundreds of Realtor websites. Keep it simple, and they'll appreciate it.

Explain who you are, what you do, and how to reach you. Feel free to include a tagline that tells people what your specialty is; for example, *residential real estate in Rye, New York.*

If you want people to respond, put a register button on the top right hand side of your front page. The eye seems to go there. That's a good place to test an offer, too. You might test your free newsletter and then let viewers click through to an easy-to-register form. Don't forget to mention when they'll begin to receive the newsletter.

Our general manager found his home in Connecticut

When Dwain Jeworski came from Canada to work with us in our New York offices, he had to find a home for his family in a very short time. He decided on Connecticut, ran an MLS search, and found Bob Mori at www.TeamMoriRealEstate.com.

Bob Mori of RE/MAX then was able to enter Dwain's criteria into an automatic program and send Dwain all the listings that fit his needs within half an hour of posting them. When we moved the company to Florida, Bob Mori set Dwain up with an agent down here, and Dwain bought his next home that way.

Bob Mori has a wonderful relationship-building technique. He stays in touch with prospects and previous buyers with a series of e-mails filled with helpful ideas about buying homes in Connecticut. Bob could have his e-mails sent automatically, but he told me he likes to personalize many of them instead. He stays in contact with about 2,400 people. His goal is to close between 3 and 5 percent a year or up to 120 sales. Not bad.

When I interviewed Bob, he said *"I treat every e-mail as a lead I can't live without, so I have to respond to it immediately. The immediacy is vital because the prospect had a question in mind, and soon afterwards they forget about it. Fast response is a must."*

Bob and Judy Mori's website welcomes you and invites inquiries.

What Is the Easiest Way to Set Up a Website?

Get someone else to do it. At least get help. I called Teresa King Kinney, CEO of RAMB, Realtor® Association of Greater Miami and the Beaches. She told me that her association provides a property search for MLS listings, in thirteen languages, which also serves as an e-marketing tool, with a Web design set-up wizard that has the ability to link to even more languages. When I met her in person at the 2006 Real Estate Congress, she was introducing the speakers, helping attendees network with each other, and working really hard to make it a successful event for everyone. She's managed to have alliances with fifty associations around the world, offering education and marketing tools on the website and various expos, events, and trade missions. If you're located in the South Florida area, check out www.Miamire.com. If not, someone in your neck of the woods offers a similar service (for state and local directories, check the National Association of Realtors® website). See RAMP website on page 59.

If you really want to do it yourself, spend some time in a good book store. I recommend the *Idiot's Guide* and the *For Dummies* series. If I can understand them, anyone can.

Your Website Is Like a Store

People love it when they're not being "sold at" all the time. I guess that's why Coldwell Banker won the Web Marketing Association's best real estate website award last year. Their winning website features a friendly make-believe pooch, a Personal Retriever® who asks you what you're looking for in a property, and then e-mails you some ideas. The dog is fun and not at all threatening; he won't hound you with calls, or show his face everywhere barking, "Call me for listings." This kind of idea works wonders.

*Maybe you can have a live agent available either
online or on the phone*

Modern communications systems are astounding, and I strongly recommend that you try to take advantage of every opportunity they offer. For example, as Mark Weithorn mentioned, you and a prospect can be thousands of miles apart, talking on the phone or

Home page of Realtor® Association of Greater Miami and The Beaches (RAMB), which has many resources and links for its members.

chatting online in a separate dialog box, as you review a property together. Lands' End does that with its online catalog. People can call up and tell the representative what page they're on so they can both look at it together. It lifts sales and the conversation—personal, one-to-one contact—provides invaluable database-able information. If you are not ready for that, you might consider:

1. Questions and answers about real estate in your area. List real questions people have asked you and the answers you've given.
2. A search feature for your MLS listings—many associations provide that service.
3. E-mail response to questions within 24 hours.

4. Your telephone numbers so visitors can call with questions.
5. Include some short testimonials, real ones.

Just keep it simple. We've designed a site for the, so far, fictitious Lois Geller Realty. It is uncluttered and simple to use. I did put my own face in there, but if this was a real website, I'd probably use a

This website features easy navigation and offers something relevant to prospects.

new brand. Also, create it around your customers' needs; it's not about you, it's about them.

I interviewed Karen Duncan, who works with Zeckendorf Marketing LLC at the property at 15 Central Park West. Their collateral materials are amazing; they're oversized, they continue the brand, and they show a beautiful typeface, similar to the *New Yorker*.

The website is one of my favorites. It shows the building, the views including Central Park and the courtyard, the services, and so on. Then you can select your apartment, and the building revolves to show you your exposure. Then you select the exterior, and you see the floor plan. It is worth your time to visit the website, www.15cpw.com. In the meantime, see the preview on page 62.

Brad Inman is doing something unique . . .

When I attended the 2006 Real Estate Congress, Brad Inman was a speaker. He is founder of Inman News, a leading independent real estate news service and content provider to 250 U.S. newspapers and 50,000 websites.

He talked about marketing homes in the Internet age. Then he showed a film about a house he was marketing and told the stories of the wonderful things that happened there. He specializes in original video content via the Internet.

If you are listing a home that was owned by Marilyn Monroe or Katherine Hepburn or some oil tycoon, the stories that happened there, around the pool or in the library, are wonderful tales the house can't tell someone who simply views it. Brad Inman brings the story to life by producing original video content that can be shown on a single website, or many. (You can view Brad Inman's site at www.inmanstories.com.)

Privacy and security are serious issues

People are worried that they will have problems with their personal information when they provide it online. So you should consider a privacy policy and post it on your website. Maybe something like this: *We will not provide your personal information to other companies without your permission.* People won't provide much information online unless they believe your site is secure.

15 Central Park West's website features a wealth of information about the area and the building, including an "inside look."

E-mail Marketing

A few years back, all of our clients told us that they wanted to do less expensive snail mail and more "free" e-mail. At first glance, this looks like a no-brainer. There's no postage on e-mail. Nothing to print. No lettershop. You get results back quickly, so you can try all kinds of different ideas and fine tune your campaign. There's no down side.

Hoo boy.

We talk about this all the time in our seminars because people are fascinated with the combined idea of unlimited reach and low, low cost. A few years ago, Mike McCormick, our creative director, started asking "Has anyone here ever bought something as the result of an unsolicited e-mail from a company they don't know?" So far, not one hand has gone up.

E-mail is not a good prospecting tool. It is, however, a great relationship tool if you already have the relationship established.

Low cost? Nope. Professional e-mail campaigns take a lot of work (and you do want a professionally staged program.) We use an e-mail provider at Mason & Geller and the cost is 1 to 2 cents per name, and these are my own names.

It also takes time and money to put together the creative (words and images) in an e-mail message. It matters how the e-mail looks, and the words are crucial. You can't just go on and on as you can in postal mail. You can't use the same kind of words because, for some reason nobody fully understands yet, what works in regular mail usually doesn't work in e-mail.

When you get a response via regular mail, you can take a day or two to reply. In e-mail, you must respond almost immediately. There's something about online commerce that demands immediate gratification.

E-mail bugs a lot of people. It helps to remember that you compose your e-mail in isolation. There's just you and your one message, and that message is very important to you. But your prospects and clients don't care all that much, and they see your e-mail in their computers' inboxes which are usually just jammed by all kinds of marketers plus, of course, spammers and scammers. It's also important to remember that people sitting at a computer are usually there for a reason: to work, play, or communicate with friends. They're not sitting there waiting for an unsolicited e-mail. It is so easy to hit that little deleting X. E-mail has no substance to it. No dimensions, no front and back. It's not a tactile thing you can feel. It is very easy to dismiss.

From and **Subject** are vital in e-mail. They're the first thing your recipients see, and if they don't like the From and Subject, they'll delete the whole thing, unread.

The real beauty of the Internet (and e-mail) is that it brings us closer to our prospects and clients and helps us provide them with a level of service that can surprise and delight them. Prospects can look at homes on your website and ask you questions, you can e-mail them directions and find them more possibilities all in minutes. It's a whole new creative world for you. If you're a small company, you can act big, and if you're a big company, you can be "human" enough for a one-to-one relationship with every prospect.

The Gold in Your Database

If knowledge is power, then your prospect and customer database can give you the power to go beyond making a good living all the way to making a great living.

Let's begin with what your database is to you. At its most basic, it's a list of all your contacts:

- Clients who have listed their homes with you
- Clients who have purchased from you
- Prospects who have worked with you or are currently shopping with you
- Other referrals/friends/contacts who are part of your network

Of course, you already have these contacts in your PDA (e.g., Palm Pilot, Treo, etc.), which serves as your phone book, calendar, and portable mind — but are you really using it? You know there is gold in there somewhere, but where?

The gold is likely back in the office buried in data, in notes, on three-by-five cards, or in various Microsoft Word files. It is the kind of data that tells you the crucial details about the names in your PDA, such as:

- Why are they moving?

  ○ They are moving for employment relocation. They want to move (additional bedroom, better schools)
  ○ If the right deal came along, they would move

- What is their timeframe?
- Price range?
- Demographics (age, kids, etc.) and Psychographics (what they like to do/habits)?
- What is most important to your customer in a move?

  ○ Schools
  ○ Proximity to work
  ○ Floor plan
  ○ Community amenities

- Who is going to be impacted by this move?

  ○ Children
  ○ Parents
  ○ Grandparents

This is the data that you already instinctively use as you build relationships with prospects and customers, one at a time. Database marketing is a way to automate that process, an important piece of your marketing; it allows you to target each prospect/customer, hundreds or thousands at a time, with individually relevant messages. The result: more listings, more sales, and more fun, because you'll be working smarter, not harder. It'll be more fun because you'll find the gold by using your time more effectively. If done correctly, your database will connect you with eager prospects. But there is some work to do. First, you need to keep your database current, updating it after you talk with customers. Second, you need to develop an ongoing relationship strategy with your prospects. And third, you need to communicate in a relevant way to each prospect.

Tools of the Trade

Let's start with a PC (personal computer). You need one. In fact, you use one every day, and you will be using it even more in the future. For all those digital pictures you take, this is not the place to skimp. What do you need? I vote for speed. Faster is better. More memory and storage help too! For around $800 to $1,000, you can buy a notebook computer with the following characteristics:

- Intel Pentium M processor (or better)
- Microsoft Office software
- Microsoft Windows XP
- 60 gigabytes (GB) hard drive
- 512 megabytes of RAM
- Internal wireless 802.11 b/g networking for internet access
- 24x CD burner/DVD combo
- Anti-virus software (Norton, McAfee, or from your Internet service provider)

As quickly as this book goes to print, you'll see even better buys than this. My recommendation is to go to www.Dell.com (they'll put it together for you or www.bestbuy.com) to start your shopping process; if you're uncomfortable in this space, recruit a teenager to help you, as that will get you rolling. Teenagers know all the latest gizmos on computers, not to mention that they type like the wind. I suggest that you buy the warranty support, especially if you get a portable notebook computer. On many models, the batteries have a short lifespan, and the display panels seem to malfunction at high rates. Your clients have also been known to spill coffee and other liquids on the keyboard, and these machines are unforgiving. *Consumer Reports* recently endorsed warranties for these products, so consider this option seriously.

Using Excel, Word, Access, and Outlook

Let's take a look at how you manage your listings and leads today. For starters, you may be like many real estate agents I have met with files scattered everywhere, maybe a notebook or two full of notes, business cards floating here and there. Sound familiar? Is it hard to find stuff when you really need to? Well, you are not alone. Microsoft has been trying for years to find a way to make it easier to organize information, and I bet they'll figure it out. But for now, the burden is on you to get organized.

Spreadsheets can help you maintain lists of contacts, but as the number of rows and columns grows, life quickly becomes miserable. Microsoft Access offers relational database capabilities that allow you to keep your contacts organized, and it links nicely with Microsoft Word so that you can mail out letters and maintain a dialogue with contacts. But Access requires some programming capability, and you are required to build in all of the contact management and time management functions.

The best answer is to go with a packaged solution that can help you manage every aspect of your business.

Lead Management Solutions

There is one truth about systems to help you manage contacts: You get out of them what you put into them. Leading sales executives tell me that their highest performers are those individuals who use contact management systems to their full potential.

If you work for a large real estate company, then you may be using one of the major sales force automation systems, such as ACT or Salesforce.com. Both of these systems offer easy-to-use contact management solutions, but they need to be customized for the real estate business.

Some entrepreneurs have done this already. When I Googled "real estate contact management systems," Google returned 76,000,000 matches on the Web. In other words, there is no shortage of software companies eager to offer their services to you. So where should you begin to look for a packaged solution?

Your shopping list should include the following capabilities:

- Contact management
- Listings management
- Activity planning
- E-mail campaign management

There are two solutions that seem to be gaining favor, particularly for start-up real estate businesses:

- AgentOffice (www.realtystar.com)
- Top Producer (www.topproducer.com)

Both of these systems offer a full range of capabilities to help you get started. You can choose from countless systems that build upon ACT and Microsoft Outlook. When you choose a system, live by it! It will improve your productivity beyond your wildest dreams.

MLS Information: How Can I Use It to Market to Customers?

Most Realtors are very familiar with the multiple listing services. The information that you enter into the MLS is the information that can help drive your prospecting efforts. By capturing the key information from your listings in a database, you can match listings to your prospects' requests using systems similar to the ones mentioned above, and you can automatically e-mail them the listings that might interest them. Key elements include:

- Bedrooms
- Square footage
- Bathrooms
- Lot size
- Year built
- School district

One real estate company with a great e-mail program is located at www.ziprealty.com. As new listings arrive that meet clients' specified needs, the company automatically sends out e-mails from their designated agent, roughly once a week for contacts they are not working with otherwise. A picture of the agent is posted in the return address portion of the e-mail, helping to personalize the communication. Now, think about the cost to the Realtor. It is almost free to send out this communication (some service providers charge a penny or two for each e-mail sent), depending on the service you use; yet if one of your prospects chooses to purchase from you, it is worth several thousand dollars in commission.

Using the Web

According to the National Association of Realtors®, over 70 percent of all people who purchase a home today use the Internet as part of their search, and that number has grown steadily over the past five years. Most consumers expect a realty website, and there is a wide range of custom developers who can build one for you. For under $1,000, you can have a website with the following features:

- Just listed/just sold information
- Your newsletter
- All your listings with photos of the exteriors and interiors
- A function to allow prospects to ask for additional information
- Tips on selling/buying homes
- Collection of referrals to build your database

Consider the following links to service firms to help you get started:

- www.AgentImage.com
- www.ihouseweb.com
- www.RapidListings.com
- www.webpak.com

Finding the Gold: Creating a Recipe for Success

To be successful in finding the gold, you need a few noteworthy ingredients. First, keep your website and database as simple as possible. That may sound basic, but large companies fail every day in this area, because the process they created is too much of a burden for the organization.

Second, live by the rules that you set at the beginning of this process, particularly around the need for entering data. Your database is of limited value if it is not up-to-date. Discipline separates success from failure in this area. Create a standard lead form that allows you to collect the same information from every prospect, and stick to it.

Third, an ounce of prevention will reduce your stress level significantly. Backup your database and website at least once a week to CDs, DVDs, or another computer. Everyone has a personal computer crash at some point, and you will not be the exception. Expect it, and be ready to recover.

Finally, keep a sense of humor throughout this process. Things going wrong is part of doing business. Your computer will crash, you will lose data, you will be frustrated along the way. But perseverance will be rewarded by the smiles of your satisfied customers and the increase in your commissions. The gold is there, and your database provides a key resource for finding it and executing direct marketing strategies.

Marketing with Your Contact Database

Dwain Jeworski

Your database, that information-packed list of prospects and customers, is your best and most manageable source of future business. It's also a great tool to keep marketing costs under control, because it will give you a higher response rate than purchased lists, and that, in turn, will improve your ROI (return on investment).

It takes time to create a good marketing database, and it should be looked at as the next step in marketing to rented lists. Converting people from rented lists into contacts is a good way to grow your database. Plan your lead-generating marketing programs with this goal in mind, using offers that entice people at least to get on your list, even if they aren't going to buy anything right away.

Many agents use lead generation (totally new business) as their *only* way to get listings or make a sale. They miss out on the opportunities a well-maintained marketing database provides. We want people to engage with us, and lead generation should be used for what it is—*generating leads to be added to your database*. If you can make an immediate sale, great, but think of it as gravy.

Once you have a reasonably sized (manageable) and organized database of (potentially) interested leads, you'll do well if you follow these basic principles:

Create pockets of interest in your database

To make the most of a database and to get better response, you need to communicate with the people most likely to be interested in your message. You manage this by *segmenting* your list into the different groups you want to target.

Common elements for segmenting lists include

1. Price range of current home—nearest $50,000 works
2. Type of current home
3. Size of home
4. Length of time in existing home, year purchased
5. Status: buyer, seller, prospect?
6. Interest: investment, move-up, local market conditions
7. School: elementary, middle, high, etc.
8. Status of contact: hot, warm, cold
9. Rent/own
10. Communication preference: e-mail, mail, phone

To get accurate information for segmenting, input this data when you create the contact. This can be easily managed with a checklist of questions when you make your initial contact. This makes it easy to work the questions into the conversation, and you won't forget to get the information you'll need to serve the prospect. An online form structured to capture the important information will do the same for people logging onto your website. People typically like to talk about themselves, so this shouldn't be a difficult process.

Surveying your contacts each year is a great way to update the information. It also shows people that you're interested in helping them. You can flag responders as warm, hot, or cold depending on responses. Just because they responded, you know they may be interested in doing business with you. People who don't respond can be considered cold, although you should try the survey again in a few weeks.

Create opportunity through communicating with the segments

Let's say you have a new listing in an area near an elementary school: a 2,400-square-foot two-story, near schools, priced at $350,000. You want to let people who may be interested know about this property, so you plan an e-mail and a postcard (for the contacts you don't have e-mail addresses for).

The people who are most likely to have an interest in this home are those that live nearby, have been in their existing home for two years or longer, own a home priced within $100,000 of this home, or have children in elementary school. You would select the audience by choosing these segments from the above list:

1. Within price range of $200,000 to $300,000
2. In current home two years or longer
3. Current home is smaller than 2,500 square feet
4. Live in same or surrounding ZIP code

Export each of the four matching look-ups and then combine all into one group. (The names will need to have duplicates removed, as you will have overlap.) Then, using contact preferences, you split the list into mail or e-mail and send out the appropriate communication.

To measure the effectiveness of your segmenting, try adding other lists into the mix. One could be rented names, and the other would be a segment of your database that was not chosen.

Getting results

Every communication that you send must have an offer. If you don't ask for a response, you won't get one. Ask yourself "Why would someone respond?" Then provide the answer. It is extremely important that you have a *call to action*, in order to find out what works. The offer is how you measure response when you track properly.

Sometimes this is done through the naming of the call to action — *July Special, Investors Insight, Market Watch*, or something similar. You'll notice that the offers are based on providing information. As agents' commissions are always under pressure, this is a good way to differentiate yourself. Homeowners like to be informed of market conditions, and offers of information let you segment prospects by their interests; then you can validate the segmentation by the response.

Asking for a response implies that you will follow-up

Plan on managing the response before you send anything out. Each response needs to be acted upon and noted in your database. You'll need to create informational pieces for follow-up. These can be in the form of newsletters, listing information, or ongoing information specific to the prospect's interest, so be ready to create these pieces. There are many agent programs out there to generate these, so adapt the offer to the ones you'll be using.

The elements of success in database marketing

1. Accurate information—Complete address, e-mail, and contact history. You can't succeed if your communications aren't being delivered. Export and run your database through NCOA at least once a year. *NCOA* (National Change of Address) is a database owned and updated by the United States Postal Service, containing permanent change-of-address records filed with the USPS over the last 48 months. Many companies specialize in this, and they are easy to find on the Web. Make sure you can give the NCOA a copy of your database, in the format of your software, and ask that they return it to you in the same format. This makes the updating easy and avoids duplication of names. Remember that when people change their addresses they often change their e-mail addresses too. Updating the e-mail address is a manual process and a good reason to contact the person.

2. A way to group lists into segments—Plan ahead of time, so your contact management system has the ability to allow you to put people in specific groups. Knowing which groups you want to focus on is the start. If you set up the groups ahead of time, you'll be able to toggle the group, avoiding data input errors. You'll also be able to quickly select a group for marketing opportunities as they arise.

3. A way to record response—Include a field for *status*. This way you will be able to pull lists based on hot/warm/cold. You'll also know which contacts to focus your energies on.

Database marketing allows you to communicate with relevance. Knowing details about people and making sure they know you will give you a step up on the competition. Being a source of timely real estate information is the best way to stand out in today's real estate market. Over time, you'll be creating a valuable asset to your clients, and that will be a valuable asset to you.

In database marketing:

- The ultimate communication is one to one, on a personal level. Be sure to put as much information as you can into your database, so you can speak to prospects and past customers "on a knowledge level."
- The main objective in direct marketing is to mail less and get a better response.
- Keeping in touch with your past customers and prospects keeps you "top of mind" when they want to buy or sell a property.
- Your database needs to be updated often.
- If you segment your file, you can send out communications to people on an ongoing basis, depending on when they want to buy or sell their properties.
- With a database in place, the whole world can be your prospects.

Direct Mail Creative

Direct mail is a great way to prospect for new business, buyers or sellers. Every real estate person I've spoken to uses direct mail and all of us get lots of it.

Plenty of studies have demonstrated that just about everyone goes through their mail the same way, using a kind of triage technique: (1) Some mail they keep automatically—bills, letters from Aunt Sadie, etc.; (2) Some they chuck in the round file instantly (and trust me on this—when six real estate agents' postcards land in the same mailbox on the same day, they all get chucked); (3) Some mail is on the bubble, could go either way

Some mailers try to get tricky, thinking they can fool people into believing a mailing is a bill, a letter from the government, or even a letter from a friend. If the envelope is cleverly

> camouflaged, people will open it. Of course, 99.99999999
> percent who do open these scuzzy envelopes realize right
> away that they've been fooled, and they get mad. This is not
> a good technique.

You're never going to make it into the automatic keeper pile.
And you certainly want to avoid the chuck-it-instantly pile. The
best you can do is get into the on-the-bubble file. Then comes the
real moment of truth. Your mailer has about a half-second to grab
the recipient; otherwise it joins the chuck-it-instantly stuff.

You can grab the recipient with fancy graphics or no graphics at
all. You can have a super-cool headline. You can have a nifty direct
mail format. That all helps, but none of it matters unless it all
comes together to answer the reader's immediate question: *What's
in it for me?* And this is just to get the envelope opened!

Our basic approach here at Mason & Geller is that the purpose
of the envelope is to get opened by someone in the mood for what's
inside.

How do you accomplish this?

Start with your own personality—who you are—your own
brand. If you work for a large company like ReMax, Century 21,
Prudential Douglas Elliman, or Corcoran, you already have a
known brand. These companies spend millions of dollar getting
people to remember their brands.

On the other hand, most people have never heard of (or have
forgotten) almost all the brands in the country. I walked through
Home Depot last night and saw about 15 branded products that
were completely new to me. Maybe the products are great, but I
never heard of them. I've heard of Coca Cola, McDonald's, Ford—
those names resonate with me, because I've used them over the
years and can see the arches stand out, even when I'm in Bangkok.
Same goes for Starbucks.

Well, if you don't have deep pockets, how can you connect with
your target market and make your brand memorable? The best
way to do this is to develop a mentality in your company of "not
selling" to people.

Back when I was running the direct marketing course at New York University, I had asked my creative director, Mike McCormick, to talk to the class. He asked a question "What is the purpose of a business?" Hands shot up and we heard the same answer from everyone, "To make money."

Mike smiled, listened, and then said "Nope. The purpose of a business is to get and keep customers." Well, you never heard such an uproar. Mike let it die down and then calmly explained, "A company can't survive unless it makes money, just as you can't survive unless you breathe. Would you say that the purpose of your life is breathing? Would you agree, that if you just live, you will breathe? If companies can learn to get and keep customers, they will make money."

The students calmed down and we had a great discussion. Changing the focus from making money to getting and keeping customers changes the way you think about business. It changes everything you do. And it gives you the opportunity to be a great marketer. For one thing, you start thinking about everything from the customer's perspective. For another, you start thinking long term.

A big part of that thinking revolves around something very natural. All other things being more or less equal, people buy from people they like and respect. Think about your own day-to-day purchases: You have a favorite coffee shop, bar, restaurant, barber, hairdresser, dry cleaner. You go back to these businesses over and over. Why? They look after you, but mostly because you like the people who work there.

Years ago, Hertz was working on a new campaign, and the company president spoke with the agency's creative director. He said, "Listen, I don't want us to talk about how great our cars are, how fast our service is, our great rates. That's the price of admission, and any company can duplicate that. I want people to like us."

We don't like people who are always selling at us. I once attended a sales seminar with a brilliant speaker who spoke of a four-pronged strategy:

1. Don't have all the answers at your fingertips, just talk, and most of all, listen.
2. Tell prospects "I don't know, but I'll find out" and then find out and follow up.

3. Confess that you may not have the right product (or property), but if you can be allowed to ask a few questions . . .
4. "Always be leaving" which means you're not cornering the prospect. You just want a few minutes to ask a few questions, and then you're out of there. Of course, this might well result in you sitting there for hours and ultimately making a sale. This kind of stuff is disarming, even charming, and people like it.

The kind of people who are always selling at me come and go from my life, but the people who help me out, give me suggestions, get me the right answers, listen to what I need, etc., are the kind of people I buy from, and they tend to stay with me forever. We call this relationship *building*, and it's why direct marketing works.

Put a human face on your company

That doesn't mean you have to use your photograph on the direct mail package, but you can humanize your brand and your services. This can be done by demonstrating human qualities like humor, understanding, generosity, and helpfulness. We receive many direct mail pieces from real estate agents, and recently we sat down in our conference room and reviewed dozens of postcards, solo mailers, and catalogs we've received.

Many of the postcards looked the same, and we couldn't remember most of them two seconds after we'd seen them. One stood out: It came from an agent in Los Angeles. He looked human, had a strange offer, and showed an animal on his piece. His name is Simon Salloom, and he works for Coldwell Banker in Los Angeles. His postcard read "Simon says, Calling all animal lovers! Buy or sell with me and enjoy a free photo session with you and your pet!" See his postcard on the next page.

That "Simon says" is memorable. His offer is believable, different, and doable. The image shows a photo of someone taking a photograph of Simon and his dog. On the reverse side he talks about the challenge of selling a home, and the fact that he's up for the challenge. There's another photo of him and a separate one of his dog.

Another of his cards has a photo of Simon sitting on a bus bench, with the headline, "Simon says, It takes more than your Realtor's face on a bus bench to sell your home." On the reverse, he

Simon "connects" with prospects with a new and different kind of offer.

talks about the challenge of selling homes today and shows four homes and apartments he's sold. There's also a "Just Listed Apartment."

Simon has developed a brand that welcomes people to call him with their listings. When I called, he told me that he's doing great, and he's only been in real estate for a short time. When I told him how much we liked his human touch, he let me know he'd considered making his pieces a bit more formal and maybe taking himself out of them. I told him to continue his great brand.

Simon continues his "Simon says" brand campaign. He is friendly and approachable.

All brands need to be consistent, so when people see your ad or direct mail piece or leave-behind, everything should have the same look and feel.

Make yourself memorable

I met Diane Silverman many years ago. She's worked in the direct marketing industry for decades. When she worked in Doubleday's list marketing department for twenty years, she used photographs of her Scottish Terrior, Duffy, to represent the Military Book Club. Sometimes he appeared in ads wearing a helmut and dog tags, and the creative team handled his costumes and props. Her dog ran in ads from 1990 to 1997.

Then after two job changes, Diane became bored with the business and met a friend who extolled the creativity of working in real estate. She also mentioned Keller Williams Realty, a company that stands behind their agents and lets them create their own "companies," which you might call brands.

Diane's an agent now in Ossining, New York, and she uses her own unique postcards to get business. She has a series of one a week for five weeks. The strategy is "Overcrowded? Time to move!" Each week there are more dogs and on the back of the postcards are free offers. The mailings have been very successful in terms of name recognition (and several leads and clients), and she's received great feedback on her business and her new dog, Disney. See page 84.

Our art director, Pepper Huff, came up with another strategy by bringing Diane Silverman's face into the creative and then making an illustration of her. Then he went one step further by showing the property as well. Maybe a bit ambitious for one effort. And yet, when we looked at them, they worked. Plus, there was something about Diane, as she is a walker and a runner in the neighborhood, which made her "memorable" in her area. See page 85.

When I went to my apartment in Miami Beach yesterday, a whole slew of postcards fell out of the mailbox. One of them said, "You know how much you love this location; don't you have a friend who would love to live here too?"

The photo shows the building and the interior of an apartment in the building. It opened up a much better connection to ask for a friend than to say "apartment available in this building."

Just-in-time mailings are interesting. They may be relevant to the prospect . . . Now that your family is growing, you might be interested in a new home. Or, now that your children are leaving the nest, you might want to consider an easier-maintenance way of life with a townhouse. See page 86.

Or timeliness can mean simply the time of year. A postcard might wish "Happy Valentines Day" on the front, and on the back show the agent's available listing. Maybe you're supposed to consider buying your valentine a new condominium? I'm not sure about that one. Another one says, "Happy Mother's Day." See page 87.

*Diane Silverman's postcard campaign gained her name recognition and aware-
ness in her neighborhood and surrounding buildings.*

This postcard features the house but still captures the agent and her dog.

This approach shows the agent as a cartoon figure because it is easier to show her running with her dog.

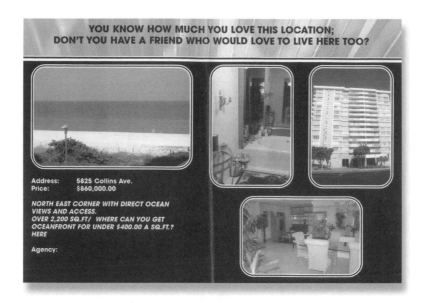

This is a good way to ask for a referral.

Solo mailings (full direct mail packages with envelope, letter, brochure, response device) almost always pull a higher response rate than postcards. Once people have become involved in opening your mail piece and reading the different elements, they're more likely to respond to it. Besides, the full DM package gives you a lot more room to develop a personality, tell a story, and push all the buttons until you hit the right one. The letter is the most important element, especially when it appears to be a personal letter. The other day, I received an agent's letter in a red envelope. It read:

> *Dear Mr/Ms. Lois K. Geller,*
>   *Hello! I am your new neighbor! I have moved my real estate business office down the block from you at . . .*

She went on about how she knows a lot about my building because she has friends and relatives who live there; then she closed with this paragraph:

> *My reputation in the industry speaks for itself.*

If you're wishing folks a happy holiday, make it relevant to buying a proposal.

What a strange thing to say! Trite, boasting. The letter started okay but it was all about her and not enough about me, the prospect. If she wanted it to be personal, she could have written to me, Ms. Lois K. Geller.

Another letter read *Dear Geller – family* and then kept switching typefaces to say a dozen different things like *We will sell your property fast and at the HIGHEST PRICE.*

The letter looked sloppy; the type was printed over the letterhead and featured a large pink flamingo. The problem with this letter is that it is not directed to me (to anyone), and good letters are *personal* (the sender knows something about me), not just *personalized* (with my name).

Maybe you can test some creative ideas that are not similar to what you and others have done in the past. I sat down with Pepper Huff, my art director, and we created some new kinds of letters for you to consider.

Letter Number One: Invitation to an open house and the beginning of relationship building by offering a thank-you gift of Emily's Chocolates. (You don't make this offer to everyone, just to people most likely to want to do business with you.) It also helps paint a picture and tell a story about the property, bringing the reader into a fantasy: *"Everyone has a dream house. It is the home you jog past in the morning that makes your heart flutter . . ."*

Riverside
Real Estate
123 Elm Street
Riverside, NY 12345-1234
1-800-123-1234

Dear Neighbor:

Everyone has a dream house. It is the home you jog past in the morning that makes your heart flutter just a bit faster as you conside how wonderful it would be to live in it.

We have a lovely house (pictured above) that is definitely someone's dream home. Maybe it is yours, or you know someone who wants to be in the neighborhood, and you can let them know.

This weekend we are having an Open House on Saturday from 11am to 2 pm, at 111 Maple Street. Please come over and say "hello" and walk through the house and see some of its beautiful features, including the new granite countertops in the kitchen, the spacious den that looks out over the deck and cherry blossom trees in the garden.

I hope to see you there!

Barbara
Barbara Smith

P.S. When you visit the open house mention you received this invite and one of our agents will give you a thank you gift of Emily's Chocolates.

This open house invitation is in a letter and offers chocolates as a thank you gift.

You can see here that this copy appeals to your prospect better than all your credentials, your photograph, your "just sold" or "just listed" copy. The copy is about *the prospect,* and that is what makes it engaging.

Letter Number Two: Getting to know you. This letter is written to set up a database of people who may be hot, cold, or warm leads for selling their properties. It's targeted to people with whom you can begin a relationship once you know something about them.

It begins with copy that already acknowledges that the writer knows something about the recipients. *You are living in a beautiful area of Ft. Lauderdale and I'm hoping that you will take a few minutes of your time to fill out my survey . . .*

The letter then offers a gift to people who spend time filling out the survey—a pen with a radio in it (great for hurricane season).

You can then database all the information from the surveys and begin to mail people a newsletter, or a direct letter if they mentioned that they are interested in selling their property soon. You might call them about that opportunity as well. See page 90.

Letter Number Three: What do you think it is worth? This letter appeals to all of us who are curious about what our friend's home is worth and the value of our own homes (so we can figure out our own net worth). This letter doesn't scream **Call us now for a free evaluation!** Instead it talks about this nice fellow named Gary Johns who can visit you and tell you the value of your home, even if you might just want to update your homeowner's insurance. He'll also bring you a gift when he visits (the offer).

The letter's objective is to begin the relationship by giving your prospect two things first, the evaluation and the gift book covering the same subject. See page 91.

Letter Number Four: Far away folks. Letter Number Four is written to people up north who might be relocating to the South for any reason: children have left for college or marriage (empty-nesters), for instance. The letter is targeted to exactly that list. It is a homey approach, and the agent (whom we've named Steve Jones) promises to bring some of his wife's maple syrup when he comes over for the visit. This is the letter to begin a relationship with a possible prospect.

Suncoast
Realty
123 Las Olas Blvd
Ft. Lauderdale, FL 12345-1234
1-888-123-1234

Dear Neighbor,

You are living in a beautiful area in Ft. Lauderdale, and I am hoping you'll take a few minutes of your time and fill out my survey. A postage-paid envelope is enclosed for you to return it. When I receive your completed survey, I'll send you a great pen that I use myself. It is unique with a radio in it (worked well in the hurricanes last year), and it is my way of thanking you.

The survey is below. Just fill it out and tear it off, and mail it back to me. I am using the information to help my clients who are looking for real estate in this area. Of course, if I can help you in any way...I'd like that too. Just call me.

All the best,

Bob

Bob Jones

B O B   J O N E S   S U R V E Y

Name _____

Address _____

City _____ State _____ Zip _____

Telephone number_____

How long have you lived in this area? __ 1-3 year __ 4-6 years __ 7-10 years __ All my life

What do you like most about your neighborhood?_____
_____

Are you considering moving to another home?_____

When would you be interested in moving? _____

Are you interested in investment property _____

Do you know anyone in the area who is relocating? _____

Name_____

Thank you for your help.

A survey letter helps you get information about a prospect and also acts as an involvement device.

**Peachtree
Real Estate**
123 Elm Street
Atlanta, GA 12345-1234

What do you think it's worth?

Dear Neighbor:

Have you ever visited a friend's home and wondered, what is this home worth? Or, have you considered the value of your own home?

Well, you don't have to speculate any more. I have an agent that specializes in your area (Gary Johns, you might know him), and he will gladly let you know the value of your home in today's market.

Even if you are not planning on selling any time soon, it is good to know the value...even to update your homeowner's insurance. So, if you'd like Gary to stop by, just give us a call at: 800-989-7675.

When he visits you, he will bring you a special gift from our office, a book we've developed entitled, Figuring Out Your Net Worth.

All the best to you,

John

John Hayes,
President
ABC Realty Corp.

P.S. If you'd rather step in our office on Elm Street, say "hello"and I'll give you a copy of this great book.

Letter Number Three makes a home evaluation sound more like a game . . . so it might get a response.

Jones Realty
123 Elm Street • Anytown, NY 12345-1234
800-123-1234

Dear Neighbor:

The cold winters in Vermont may have been invigorating at some point in time, but maybe now the cold snaps are not as comfortable as they used to be. Some of our neighbors are moving to warmer climates (recently the Moore's moved to Georgia).

If you're considering moving south full time, or maybe for a season each year....you might want to scale down your home here.

There are many town homes that are easier to care for, and can be rented too, if you'll be travelling.

If you might be considering changing your residence in any way, maybe I can help you. I can let you know the value of your home in today's market, and what homes in other areas might cost you.

If you give me a call, I can drop by and we can talk. My wife has just put together some wonderful maple syrup from her favorite trees...I'll bring you a jar when I visit.

All the best,

Steve

Steve Jones

P.S. Bob Jones (from Valley Lane) just bought his wife a townhome in Cresent Green. I can show you similar ones there... if you're curious.

Letter Number Four sounds like it is written by a real human being. People like that.

Things to Remember

Remember to relate to potential prospects like you do your friends. If you spoke to someone in the mall last week, send a note mentioning the mall chat. Ask if they want a copy of your newsletter or one of your new books: *Evaluating the Value of Your Home.*

Continue to communicate with them over time. You might call them, ask how they liked the book, and ask whether they want you to look at their home to estimate its approximate value?

The whole relationship should flow in the same way as a new friendship. It should be natural, and you should constantly be bringing value to it. Help the prospects, and they will help you.

Remember to database everyone you meet and everyone who responds to your mailing, and keep in touch with those people who move out of your area as well. The more people you're communicating with, the better your chances that someone will want to buy or sell their property . . . or know someone who does . . . and they'll think of you!

Creative Do's for Self-Mailers and Postcards

Mailings should be relevant to the prospect.	* Personalize it, if possible (no label). * Use a live stamp. * Keep in touch with current and former clients. * Develop a style (brand) that works and stick with it. * Mail often. * Target a specific group. * Use a likeable voice and tone. * Arouse interest with the outer envelope. * Proofread for typos before sending to print. * Sign your letters (use blue ink).

Mention the benefits of working with you in the copy.	* Emphasize your value: You specialize in a certain building, waterfront, seniors, multilingual, etc. * Inform me: tell me something I don't know — "Did you know ...?"
Make it clear to avoid confusion: Use the Who, What, Where, Why, When, and How.	* Who you are and why choose you? * What is the price? * Where is the property? * Why this house (or condo, etc.)? * When is the open house? * How do I contact you?
Clean designs work all the time.	* Use interesting fonts (serif typefaces) and graphics, and be sure they are easy to read. * Make sure your photos enhance the selling points. * Avoid excess: less is more.
Show the property.	* Describe property features: kitchen, closets, back yard, pool. * Always include price. * Give the address. * Tell a story: the neighborhood, the schools, the ocean breezes, etc.
Make me an offer.	* Make it relevant: "Take part in our survey and receive a $100 Lowe's gift card!"

	* Get me involved: "You're invited! Take part in our free drawing!"
Avoid fluff—too much copy.	* Focus on the property and the client, not just you.
	* Provide pictures of clients with you if possible.
	* Always tell the truth and don't over-promise.
	* Avoid using negative words, such as "stop" and "don't."
Just sold! Send a mailing in the same building or neighborhood.	* Show the building
	* Include price
	* Issue a call to action— "Call me to price your home."

Real Estate Direct Response Advertising

A direct response advertisement is written to elicit an immediate response—a lead, a request for more information, or a purchase. The important word is "immediate. If your prospect turns the page, you've lost him. So in direct response, you want to give him a reason to respond now. There are thousands of ads for real estate in newspapers and magazines, showing properties, the agent's picture, and a description—and the only "call to action" is the telephone number, e-mail address, or website.

Each morning, I receive *The Wall Street Journal*, the *New York Post* and *The Miami Herald* at my door. Each one has so many real estate ads, and most look exactly the same, except for the property they're showing.

This advertorial is always fresh as the question and answer changes each time it runs.

Last week, I opened the *New York Post* and noticed a different kind of real estate ad. I was amazed and delighted to see it.

"Ask Reba" is a great way for this real estate agent to begin a relationship with her prospects. She positions herself as an expert (as she really is, with 22 successful years in the business), and she features a question with her answer in each of the advertisements, which she calls advertorials.

At the bottom of the ad she includes some of her featured properties. It really worked for me, so I called her, and in a New York minute, she returned my call. She told me that the ad had been running the first Wednesday of every month and had been doing very well for her. Then she told me to go to her website for a very special virtual tour at www.rpmillernyc.com

I checked the website to see the apartments, and there was a beautiful one for almost 3 million dollars. When I pressed view video tour, a wonderful British voice gave me a magnificent tour of the apartment, pointing out the features, the benefits, and the views . . . it was truly a great sales presentation. This was definitely a better way of showing an apartment than using still photos room by room.

So Reba aroused my interest in her ad, made herself an authority in real estate, sent me to her great website, and hoped that I would respond to her there. She might have tried asking me to register there for a free information booklet so that she could continue to talk to me in e-mail, over time.

Direct Response Ads versus Direct Mail

Direct response advertising (for example, in a magazine or newspaper) uses most of the same elements as a direct mail campaign, with the difference being that you have less space to get the attention of readers and get them to take action now. In fact, you probably have just a few seconds to hook a customer with a headline and graphic—before he has turned the page.

The advertisement is also competing with editorial content, other ads on the page, and possibly photographs. People tend to look at other people. So if your ad is on a page with a group of photos of people who have attended a benefit dinner, for the most part your prospects will focus on those pictures rather than noticing your ad.

This morning I opened up my *New York Post*, and saw an advertisement showing the photograph of a woman with copy about her and her dream apartment.

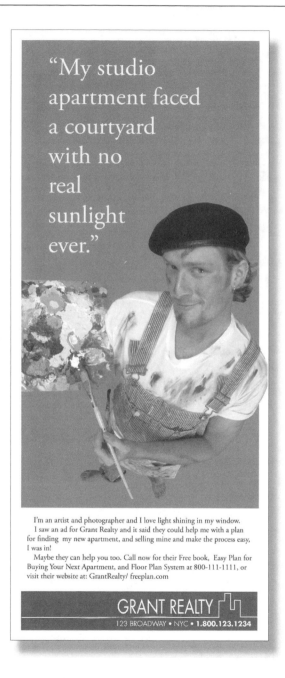

"My studio apartment faced a courtyard with no real sunlight ever."

I'm an artist and photographer and I love light shining in my window. I saw an ad for Grant Realty and it said they could help me with a plan for finding my new apartment, and selling mine and make the process easy, I was in!

Maybe they can help you too. Call now for their Free book, Easy Plan for Buying Your Next Apartment, and Floor Plan System at 800-111-1111, or visit their website at: GrantRealty/ freeplan.com

GRANT REALTY
123 BROADWAY • NYC • **1.800.123.1234**

This ad is a testimonial from a happy customer. People look at people, so it might work well.

Now, when I first saw the ad, I was delighted that one real estate company had decided to do something new and different. I liked the fact that they showed a face, and it was the face of the prospect, not a real estate agent. It was good, too, that they had decided to write the ad in her voice. Good for them, I thought.

They had promised answers to questions about buying my next apartment, but when I went to the website, there were just listings. To make an advertising campaign effective, carry through with any promise you make. The company could have provided a calculator to figure out how much you were going to make on your apartment sale, how much you could afford for the new apartment, and what you were looking for. They might have sent some suggestions by e-mail, based on the area of New York where you want to live. To show you our own idea of a different kind of ad, we've developed the one on the opposite page, using an art director's face and interests in an apartment.

Elements of Successful Direct Response Advertising

Sometimes an ad can be simple and still memorable

My cousin and his wife, Mitch and Judy Milstein, use "The Super Team" as their tagline, because they've been top producers at Long and Foster in Maryland for many years. The capes and superhero idea add up to a memorable image. Judy is a stand-up comedian, and can play off the comic image that they use.

Providing super service offers the prospective buyer or seller a real benefit in this headline, and the fact that Judy and Mitch are in the top 1 percent nationwide translates to solid performance.

Direct response advertising in real estate has three objectives:

1. To get a prospect to call, see the property shown in your ad, and buy it.
2. To build your prospect file so you can continue to communicate with the people on it, until they're ready to list or buy a property.
3. To learn something about your prospects.

To meet objective 1, you might show prospects the property they read about in the real estate ad. Even if they don't buy or rent

This ad is meant to give the prospect the security of knowing these agents are top producers.

it, but they like working with you, you might continue to show them properties until they find what they're looking for.

For objective 2, you are building a file of prospects who have already responded to you. Build a relationship with them by staying in touch, e-mailing them listings, and so on. They might begin as buyers and then also list their property with you. They might ask for your help in finding them a second home, or refer a friend to you.

Objective 3 sounds academic to people in sales, and yet it is very important. When you learn which offer works best, you save money next time you mail. You might learn that people respond best from one mailing list you never expected (see Chapter 4). You learn lots of things!

You can also learn by testing newspapers and magazines. Maybe some of these publications will let you test an A/B split of their circulation — testing one creative approach in half of their publications and another in the second half. You might want to consider two different creatives for two separate target audiences.

For instance, maybe your property is a less expensive starter home. One creative might appeal to first-time home buyers by telling them that the home might cost them the same amount of money as their current rent, and they can deduct the interest payments on their taxes.

The second creative might appeal to the seniors market and say, "Thinking of scaling down your home costs because the kids are on their own? You might want to consider this beautiful home, cost efficient in every way—electricity, land, general upkeep."

To find out what advertising space costs in publications, look them up at the library or online. Then you can call the newspapers or magazines and ask them to send you rate cards.

Why fish in the same place as all the other agents?

In direct response advertising for a property, consider where you're placing the ad. You want your ad to be in a publication that your target audience reads.

For instance, when I lived in New York, and I was searching for a new apartment, I always looked at the rental apartment ads in the classified section of *The New York Times*. The ads were organized by location—West Side and East Side—and by the number of rooms: studios, one bedrooms, two bedrooms, and larger apartments. So I'd scan the apartments for two bedrooms on the East Side and call the real estate agents about the apartment.

The New York Times and the *Village Voice* used to be the only places to find apartments in New York City, unless you had a family member in the real estate business. There are no MLS listings in the city, but there are in most other places.

Test new places to advertise. If you envision your target market, then you might consider new places to put your advertising.

Years back, I was offering Olympic commemorative coins to people who were coin collectors. I tested quite a number of numismatic newspapers and magazines, and they did marginally well in terms of sales. They didn't do *great*, however, and my boss was being challenged by the client (The U.S. Mint). I called up a few of our buyers and asked them why they'd purchased our beautiful first minting of coins.

They mentioned the ad, and told me that they were giving the coins to their grandchildren. Some of them mentioned that they'd heard that Olympic coins were very collectible. When I asked further, they said that the coins might go up in value, as the collectible pins had in past years.

So people were buying them as an investment, I thought. I decided to test the one place I knew I would find investors—*The Wall Street Journal*. Instead of talking about the collectible aspect of the coins, the ad copy talked about the investment . . . and we offered them in rolls, as we would other coins. That ad pulled a fabulous response rate, and we ran it many times in the paper.

What is the point in real estate ads?

Well, first of all, many people do buy real estate as an investment, so you might consider advertising your properties in that way, if you believe they will rise in value in the near future.

I've always been curious to see if people who read a lot might read ads more carefully than others. You might consider the "out of the box" idea of advertising your property in *The New York Times Book Review*—it might do well.

Or, if your property is on a waterfront that has great fishing, why not test a fishing magazine?

If your house is truly upscale magnificent, then advertise in the publications that feature such houses: *Architectural Digest, House & Garden, Avenue Magazine,* or the *New York Times Home Magazine.*

Your budget is a key factor in your media choices.

Of course, your first decision about where your ads will be placed is your budget. Costs vary among newspapers and magazines; usually, the larger the circulation, the higher the cost. In direct marketing we usually consider the cost per thousand. If an ad rate is $12.00 per thousand, multiply it by the number of thousands of circulation the publication has.

There are five choices for your direct response ad. When you are creating your marketing plan, compare the costs of these choices and what you believe will be your response rates. The choices are:

- Daily newspapers: The benefits of placing your ad in the daily paper are that people are used to looking for homes and apartments in the newspapers, so they know to shop there. It is also relatively inexpensive to advertise in newspapers, as you can reach many people in one area very quickly. If you get a new listing, you can write the ad, take a photo, and probably be in the paper by the weekend edition. If your listing is exclusive, even for a short time, you can then get a quick response. Targeting people who are in the same geographic area works for you as well.

- Freestanding inserts, or FSI's as they're called in the industry, are advertisements inserted into a newspaper or magazine. Most of them appear in the Sunday paper, and they tend to get noticed as they fall out, sometimes with coupon offerings. This is a vehicle to consider, as not too many real estate agents use this area of the newspaper. You can also purchase a certain quantity of the total circulation in some newspapers, just to test.

- Weekly newspapers and regional magazines are usually an inexpensive way to test your ad. I receive an Aventura publication, and often see the real estate that is being offered in my area.

- Magazines are usually quite expensive but might be worth the money if your property is a vacation place that would appeal to anyone nationally. The good thing about magazines is that you can get directly to the interests of the people who read them. In a magazine, your ad will last longer, as people hold onto magazines longer than they do newspapers. The downside is that there is a longer lead time, often a month or two, before your ad will appear. Your property would have to be exceptional to be worth the cost of placing the ad in a magazine.

- Real estate publications that appear in supermarkets are another vehicle to consider. If a property is not moving, you might consider this medium.

If everyone is using the regular classified ad size, why not test a half page? Show a photograph at an odd angle. Michael Shopenn, who is an architectural photographer, has been showing photos that are not "head-on" shots. They arouse interest, and sometimes they can welcome you into the house.

The side shot of the house shown here has the added appeal of featuring the beautiful tree in front, which makes the house look even more important.

Some ads can turn features into benefits. For example, the feature of an apartment is that it is a waterfront property. The benefit is that it has this beautiful view that is shown in the full-page ad that appeared in the *Miami Herald*. It also has a sense of urgency about it, a "call to action," because it says that Phase I of this project was sold out in record time, and the implication is that Phase II will also go quickly, so act now and get the benefit of preconstruction prices of $300,000 and up.

Sometimes ad copy can make you want to see the home, even if you've never heard of the area. That was the case when our art director, Pepper Huff, found an ad for the discriminating buyer — "Discover this private three bedroom, 3.5 bathroom residence, hidden behind a tall hedge, entering from Rivo Alto Drive. The rustic bamboo-framed gate opens to a lovely garden with a covered front porch seating area . . ." Pepper seemed to fall in love with the house, just reading the copy.

The strategy here is that you'd better hurry to see these waterfront apartments.

The property is the focal point of this ad.

Then he sat down at his computer and developed an ad for his own house in Hollywood. His approach was to give the reader a "feeling for the home" which was built in the 1950s. The design looks like the 50s with the fountain pen and the type fonts from that period. He shows views of the rooms (if you look hard, you can see George, his cat, on the chair) and a complete floor plan. He then bullet points the features, including the tiles he just completed installing.

Note that there is no photo of the real estate agent, Anne Smith. If prospects are interested in the house or the area, they can call her. It seems more dignified not to show the photo. If we included her photo, everyone would look at her face and it would distract from the property. See the ad on page 108.

When our creative team talked about real estate advertising, they said that advertisers should consider THE RULES:

1. If there is room, include a floor plan.
2. Be as clear as possible. Sometimes abbreviations can be tough to understand for the first-time buyer or for someone who hasn't looked at houses in a while. BR is bedroom, LR is living room, WC or BA is bathroom, GA is garage, and so on. In New York, ads often mention split bedrooms, which means the bedrooms are on different sides of the apartment.
3. Consider using more than one photo, maybe an exterior shot and the living room of a home.
4. Use great words, if they apply; for example, "granite" and "stainless steel," because they mean the place is up-to-date. Stay away from cozy (small), state-of-the-art (vague), fabulous (an over-promise), and exclamation points in copy.
5. Include a strong call to action: "Call John Burns at 456-7689 between 9 and 5. If you leave a message, your call will be returned in two hours."
6. Ask for good placement. Ads that are on right hand pages, as close to the front of the publication as possible, attract more attention.
7. Even though you are usually advertising one property, you are receiving leads for other properties and for use in your relationship-building campaign. Be sure you database every inquiry you get, as they might provide future leads for you or a friend.

8. Evaluate the responses you get. Whether or not, you sell or rent the property, make a list of all the places you advertise and the number of responses that you receive from each ad. If you spend money on classified advertising, track the number of people who call from those ads as well. That way you will figure out what is working for you and what isn't. Why spend money next year on something that didn't work for you for the last two years? Also, evaluate the costs of each ad you run, and then which one produced the highest profit (which ad generated a lead who eventually bought a property from you).

9. Consider broadcast media. Direct response radio and direct response television in local markets are not out of the question for you. If you want to generate a lot of excitement about you and your company and get the phones ringing, try it. Direct response radio is usually most effective around talk radio shows, as people are already listening and will tune into what you're saying. If there is a local station, it might be worth considering.

You might also want to think about providing tips on buying or selling homes, and then position yourself as the spokesperson for this radio spot.

Television has become very popular as a branding vehicle for many large Realtors. I see BuyOwner, ReMax, and Century 21 commercials every single night. If you're interested in positioning your brand in a big way, television might be the way to do it. Cable TV spots are not expensive, but you have to consider the cost of the production of the spot itself.

The TOOLS

Think about where you want to place your ads.

Who is your target market? Who is the target market for the publication you are considering?

_____

_____

_____

Are there many real estate ads in the publication?

_____

_____

Have you tested the four basic media for good response?

_____

Daily newspapers? _____

Magazines? _____

Free standing inserts? _____

Weekly newspapers? _____

Broadcast media? Radio? Television?

_____

_____

_____

Get the most for your advertising dollar:

- Use a source code to track responses to your ads.
- Request good placement—right hand page, as close to the front of the publication as possible.
- Ask about special real estate related issues of the publication.
- Track and evaluate the results.

Planning a Campaign

At our agency, Mason and Geller Direct, we do all kinds of campaigns for companies from banks to hotel chains, from product companies to catalogers — and it is always the same. When the clients walk into our boardroom, they want to talk about clever ideas, new looks for their brands, or some brilliant headline they dreamed about last night.

Direct marketing covers all of those things and one much more important element. That element is **goal setting** for each campaign.

In the first chapters of this book, you learned about lists and offers, direct mail packages and direct response advertising. Now that you understand more about those aspects of a program, you can put all the elements together in one place and develop your own real estate plan.

When you plan a campaign, write down on paper every facet of it, so you can evaluate the results at the end.

You need to write it all down so that you will think through every detail of the program before you actually start the process. This will also give you a road map to refer to at any point, to keep your ideas on track.

The plan is key to any direct marketing program. That is why companies like ours develop a lot of plans for our clients—because we need to think through every single detail, every budget item, every part of the media plan. It is work, but well worth the effort you put into it.

Your plan doesn't have to look beautiful. It can be in a spiral notebook; as long as it is always nearby for easy reference and not filed away.

Background

The first part of the plan is the "background." In the background section include relevant information about your real estate business:

- Do you handle mostly sellers? Do you mostly help buyers?
- What are the benefits of working with you? Do you have a special talent: Can you can help sellers to "stage" their houses for their sale? Are you good at pricing their properties so they sell quickly and appropriately?
- What have your clients said about you in the past? Do they love working with you because you get a good sense of what they're looking for? Do they appreciate the fact that you negotiate well for them?
- Write down your past commission structure and what you're looking for going forward—if you've been most successful selling lakefront property or if you're best at selling homes in your own neighborhood. So, if your usual commission is 6 percent of the selling price of a property, and you've been successful in your neighborhood, you'll maintain that level. If you want to break into lakefront property, you might have to ask for only 5 percent from the seller, so you can begin to establish a track record in that kind of real estate.

- What are the results of your past direct mail campaigns? What do you think has worked, and what hasn't? Attach your past ads and direct mail programs to the background section of your plan, so everything is there to review.
- Consider your competition. What are they doing in the mail and in advertising? Get samples of their pieces and put them together for review. What are they doing that is similar to what you're considering? How will you stand out as new and different from them?
- Now that you have seen other agents' mailings and ads, make a list of your own strengths and weaknesses and why people should select you over all your competitors.

Now you are probably ready for the next component of the plan . . .

Objectives

In designing a direct response ad or a direct mail program, it is a good idea to figure out what you want to happen as a result. What do you really want to accomplish?

Please don't say, "I want to make money." You need to be specific, to have a numerical objective.

Instead, you might say, "My objective is to get three new listings, with house values in the $300,000 range in my neighborhood in Long Beach, New York." Now, that is specific and probably achievable, if you mail the right number of letters, follow up with the leads, and target people who may be ready to consider selling their properties.

When you are setting up your objectives, consider your past response rates.

So, for instance, you mailed 5,000 postcards last year, received 100 responses, and half of those either bought or sold a property through your company. Consider that a beginning point. *If you decided this year that you would test letters against postcards and that you would track response more carefully, maybe you will get 120 responses; if the lists are better, you'll convert a higher percentage of people who will transact business with you.*

The Strategy

Once you know your objectives, you can then spend some time thinking about your strategy. What is your strategy? It is the big idea that takes you from objectives to tactics.

It sounds like a simple idea, and yet strategists at corporations and agencies make the big money, because it is tough work to come up with a good solid new strategy. Also, people tend to confuse strategies with tactics.

For years, at major agencies we would battle among ourselves as to what the real strategy should be. This gives you a focus, the one big idea you will use to achieve your objectives. In writing plans, often we would include many objectives but only one strategy. You may do that when you work on your plan.

Years ago we were working with Ford of Canada. They wanted to gain a larger share of women buying cars in their dealership (their objective).

The strategy we used was to develop a database of executive women who need cars and who might be in different stages of car ownership. That database would then act as a machine to let us know when the women would have the highest likelihood of buying a car — that is when we sent them an incentive to come in to the dealership for a test drive.

Another plan we worked on was for Weight Watchers. We wanted to move away from "before and after" photographs of women, and instead developed a strategy that would begin a relationship with prospects and members. The idea was to have two sketched characters, Brenda and Elaine. They talked to each other about the challenges of losing weight, just like two friends would do. The strategy was to have the prospect relate easily to the two characters, and make it easy to come in for a Weight Watcher's meeting, with special offers, recipes in the mail, and so on. It worked very well. The strategy for "Brenda and Elaine" was to build a relationship between them and our members who could identify with them. The previous "before and after" shots of people were tactics that were attention-getting, but people couldn't relate to them in the long term.

Your choice for your own real estate strategy will be based on your budget, your service, the time you can allocate to the program, and your target audience.

Tactics

The tactics that we used for the Ford campaign to get more women into the car dealerships involved building a relationship with the women by communicating with them in the mail—with letters, newsletters, and a survey that asked them when they intended to buy their next car. That was all databased; based on their answers to that key question, they could receive personalized offers when they had the highest likelihood of buying, perhaps an offer that would represent an upgrade from their current cars.

The tactics are really all the different ways you might implement the strategy. The first factor to consider is usually the budget. How much can you afford to spend to implement the strategy, against how much you are likely to make, based on your objectives?

Another thing to consider is your target market. Do you want to use your house file for referrals? Do you want to rent a list of people who might have grown children in your ZIP code? Do you want to mail one of the lists discussed in Chapter 4? Take some time and envision your best prospect. Where would you find that type of person, and on what list?

Then you can consider the creative approach you want to use. Should you use direct mail, direct response advertising? What offers do you want to test? Do you want to include photographs of properties in your mailing? Do you want to include a brochure with the letter?

When you begin your program and get responses, remember to write them all down, so that you will know which strategy worked best for your business.

Estimate of Costs

Once you've put together your objectives, strategy, and tactics, you need to know how much this will cost you. It is usually a good idea to get an estimate on the best program, the one you think will do the ultimate job for you. That means the direct mail package with the most components, or the direct response ad that has the largest space, or the radio spot that everyone in the office likes. You can always scale down that package, but if you think it will perform best for you, you might want to test it.

Once you have the estimates, figure out your break-even point

You can do that by deciding how many pieces you might mail, a possible response rate, how many responders might convert to a sale, and how much money you are likely to net from that sale.

It sounds more complicated than it really is. Let's consider this "what if" scenario:

> *If you mail 5,000 pieces and pull 1 percent response, you'll get 50 responses. Maybe 20 of them will be interested in working with you to buy or sell, and maybe 25 percent of those will buy or sell a home over a period of time. That is five people.*
>
> *For the sake of this exercise, let's say just one of the five people sells their home for $400,000, and you get 6 percent commission from that sale: that's $24,000. You probably share that commission with a buyer's agent, so you'll have $12,000. If you share that with your office, maybe you'll net out $6,000.*
>
> *If you mailed 5,000 pieces and they cost you about $1.00 each, then you paid $5,000 for the piece (including the postage).*

So if you get one listing, as we laid out, you've broken even. If the other four people decide to buy homes, you have probably made a good profit on your mailing.

In addition, there should always be a **contingency plan** and a **timetable**.

If the mailing doesn't pay for itself, what is the next step? Or, if the mailing pulls a better than projected response rate, how many more people can you mail to next month from the same list?

The timetable is important so you stay with the deadlines you write down in your plan. It is important to know that you are mailing at the best time for people to be listing or looking for properties. Of course, you also want to mail to them in between as well, so you can begin to build relationships with hundreds of people, more than you might ever expect to do in person.

The Most Important Step in Your Marketing Plan

Don't put it away. Keep it on your desk and refer to it; keep a report card for yourself about the progress you are making and the results you are getting from your efforts. If you think it is not doing so well, go back and look at your projections—you might find out you're doing even better than you planned.

Spend time now, and write your plan!

TOOLS: A Campaign Checklist

Background:

✓ Do you handle mostly sellers? Do you mostly help buyers?

_____

_____

✓ What have you been most successful selling? Single-family homes, townhouses, condominiums? Are your buyers mostly families or singles?

_____

_____

✓ What are the benefits of working with you? Do you have a special talent?

_____

_____

✓ What have your clients liked about you?

_____

_____

✓ What is your commission structure now; what are you looking for going forward?

_____

_____

✓ The results of your past direct mail campaigns: What has worked and what hasn't? Attach your past ads and direct mail programs to the background section of your plan so everything is there for you to review.

✓ Consider your competition: What are they doing in the mail and in advertising? Get samples of their pieces and put them with the background section for review. What are they doing that is similar to what you're considering; how will you stand out as new and different from them?

_____

_____

✓ Make a list of your own strengths and weaknesses and why people should select you over all your competitors.

_____

_____

_____

Objectives:

✓ Specifically, what do you want to achieve? Consider past response rates, and be realistic.

_____

Strategy:

✓ What is your "big idea" that will make the program work? For example:

- To define your targeted audience, by reaching out to new parents or empty nesters.

- To improve your database by keeping in touch with past clients and prospects.

Tactics:

✓ Develop a list plan for your newly defined target audience.

✓ Keep your database up-to-date. Check it yourself.

Ballpark Estimates:

✓ How much will it cost you to print and produce your new campaign?

Contingency Plan:

✓ What are the next steps if the campaign does not pull the response you thought it would?

✓ If the campaign generates a better response, who else can you mail to?

Timetable:

✓ How long will it take, from start to finish, to complete your plan?

✓ Clearly define your deadlines, so you know you'll be mailing at the time you're most likely to get the best response.

Use this space to draft your plan:

_____

_____

_____

_____

_____

_____

_____

_____

_____

_____

_____

_____

_____

DM Math for Real Estate Agents

If you have a copy of my book *Response!* you can read the chapter "Mail Order Math" and figure out what you need to know from there. But you'd have to wade through a lot of stuff about general direct marketing, which is mostly for companies selling things like insurance, clothes, or magazine subscriptions. Your business doesn't really fit their DM model. You need a very specialized DM math for real estate agents.

It should be pretty easy—except for your first step, which could take some work. I want you to start with a little research into your selling history (your revenue from sales), say over the past three years, so you can answer two questions:

1. On average, what's a listing worth to you? (Whether you make the sale or not.)
2. On average, how much is a sale worth to you? (Whether it's your listing or not.)

You need to go pretty deep here, because sales and listings are worth more than you might immediately suspect. For instance, you might sell a home and get a referral. Then, three years later, the people who bought the home might decide to sell, so you get the listing, *and* you get to sell them their new home.

I don't know how all that shakes out in your business, so you'll have to figure it out yourself. At least try to estimate a rule of thumb that might look something like this:

Immediate Revenue (Commissions) + 10% from referrals, resales, etc.

Why would *Time* magazine spend $5,000,000* to generate $1,000,000 worth of subscriptions?

Because they really spent the money to acquire customers, people who have demonstrated that they are willing to spend money because of a direct mail solicitation.

Time uses the subscribers to bolster their advertising rates with major media buyers. *Time* also makes money on subscription renewals, which are much less expensive and have much higher responses. They also offer gift subscriptions and subscriptions to other magazines they publish (*People, Fortune, Sports Illustrated*, etc.). They offer their book sets (*The Settling of the West*, WWII history, etc.) And they sell music (Greatest Hits of the 50s.) They also rent the lists of their subscribers to other companies and make a lot of money that way. In short, they invested for the long run.

* *$5,000,000 and $1,000,000 are fictional numbers for illustration. Time Inc. doesn't share their real numbers with me ... or anyone else.*

The topic of commissions isn't something I want to go into here except to note that they're all over the place, from 6 percent down to 1 percent. If you work for a brokerage firm, you probably get half the commission, whatever it is, and if you sell other agents' listings, you have to split with them, too (and vice versa). I even know unlicensed agents in New York who get finder's fees.

As I write this, the average selling price of a home in the United States is $220,000, so we'll use that in our examples. And 6 percent commission seems to be at least a historical standard. Let's assume you split your commissions with your company. To make it simple, we'll ignore splitting commission with other agents on the premise that whatever you lose when you sell another agent's listing, you gain when another agent sells one of yours.

All that means is that we're going to guesstimate, just for the examples in this chapter, that your average commission is 3 percent of $220,000, which comes to $6,600.

Your numbers might be quite a bit different, which is why you researched your last three years. Once you get the numbers, which will be reliable because they're based on reality, not guesswork, you're almost ready to start figuring out your *direct marketing allowable*.

Your DM allowable tells you how much you can spend on direct marketing to make a sale (or get a listing) and break even. That doesn't mean you'll just break even, though. The DM allowable is a working number, and breaking even is just a standard against which you measure results. On the surface, a DM allowable is pretty simple:

Revenue – Costs = DM Allowable

Revenue is, of course, how much money you make in the short term *and* in the long term. *Costs* are how much it costs you to make that money, *not counting the costs of your ad, commercial, or direct mail piece.* So if your average revenue on a sale is $6,600 and it costs you $400 to make the sale, you could spend $6,200 on direct marketing to get that sale, and you would break even. *PLEASE REMEMBER that the dollar figures and other numbers in this chapter are for illustration. Use your own reality-based numbers when you do your calculations.*

When you think about it, you and I are in exactly the same business. We are both building relationships . . . and selling our time. I sell my time when I develop direct marketing campaigns for Mason & Geller's clients. You sell your time when you work on buying or selling real estate for your clients. So give your time a value, say $100 an hour. How much time do you spend, on average, getting a listing or making a sale? Count every hour, including the time you spend on open houses, driving people around, visiting homeowners, preparing advertising and direct marketing programs, and other activities. Let's say you spend 25 hours to make a sale. That would be $2,500. The formula now becomes:

Revenue – (Costs + cost of time) = DM Allowable

or,using numbers

$6,600 – ($400 + $2,500) = $3,700

Now we need one more big concept before we work all this out. The big concept is called *incrementality*, a $5 nonword that just means extra sales trackable to your direct marketing efforts.

- *If you did no direct marketing, how much money would you make this year?*
- *If you spend $25,000 on direct marketing, how much more would you make?*

Let's say you would clear $100,000 this year if you just kept doing what you're doing. And then direct marketing would add, say, $25,000 in hard costs plus 50 hours of your time, which brings the total additional costs to $30,000. That means you'd have to make $130,000 to make it all worthwhile.

In other words, you'd need $30,000 in *incremental revenue* to break even. (Actually, you'd be doing a lot better than breaking even for two reasons: You'll be paying yourself $100 an hour for 50 hours of extra work, and you'll be acquiring knowledge as you go along, which, in the long run, will be worth a lot more to you.)

When you're just starting you're going to have to spend money *planting seeds* and *filling the pipeline*. Planting seeds means that part of your investment in direct marketing will go into making people aware you exist, generating feedback, and starting relationships. Filling the pipeline means copywriters, designers, printing costs, and tests. You're going to test copy and designs as well as lists, offers, letters vs. postcards, and so on. At first, you won't be getting as big a bang for your buck as you would like, because some of the things you'll be testing won't work as well as others. Let me set up a few scenarios to show you what I mean.

> *Imagine that you have three offers, three letters, two postcards, and four list sources. (See Chapter 3 about offers, Chapter 7 for information on letters, Chapter 4 about lists, and Chapter 3 about testing.) Table 1 shows how you might test them all in the mail in various combinations so you can read the results easily. This is called a test grid.*

Table 1

Test Cell	Creative	List	Offer
i	Letter 1 a	A	A
ii	"	"	B
iii	"	"	C
iv	"	b	A
v	"	c	A
vi	"	d	A
vii	Letter 2 a	A	
viii	Letter 3 a	A	
ix	Postcard 1	a	A
x	Postcard 2	a	A

This is a good start. You've guesstimated, using your sales instinct, that Letter 1, List a, and Offer A are going to give you your best results. But you're not sure; your instinct isn't 100 percent infallible, so you test.

You'll notice on the grid that only one thing changes in each test cell. In cells i, ii, and iii, we're testing the offers so the letter and the list stay the same. In cells iv, v, and vi, we're testing lists with the letter and the offer the same and in cells vii, viii, ix, and x, we're testing the "creative" approaches.

If we mail 1,000 pieces in each cell, the total will be 10,000, and it will probably cost you about $10,000. Table 2 shows a wildly over optimistic picture of what might happen.

Table 2

Test Cell	Responses	Response %	Conversions To Sale	Conversions as % of total mailed	
i	12	1.2%	4	0.4%	Test All
ii	8	0.8%	1	0.1%	Test Offer
iii	14	1.4%	2	0.2%	Test Offer
iv	16	1.6%	7	0.7%	Test List
v	12	1.2%	4	0.4%	Test List
vi	21	2.1%	9	0.9%	Test List
vii	16	1.6%	5	0.5%	Test List
viii	19	1.9%	8	0.8%	Test Creative
ix	8	0.8%	1	0.1%	Test Creative
x	10	1.0%	2	0.2%	Test Creative
	136	1.36%	43	0.43%	

Your best list is d (cell vi tells us that). Your best offer is A (cell i), and your best creative is Letter 3. So what happens when you roll out, putting these winners together: Letter 3 with list d and Offer A? Your response goes up, a lot. Probably about double.

But that's far too optimistic a scenario, especially for an initial mailing. Forty-three sales! Wow! You'd make $283,000 right off the bat plus that 10 percent we talked about earlier. You'd make over $300,000! And a 10-test grid with just 10,000 pieces mailed won't give you the reliable information you need. In everyday DM, our basic rule of thumb is that you need 300 responses to each test cell before you have more or less reliable results. But that would mean mailing over 200,000 pieces, and I didn't want to scare you. Consider the above grid and results as exaggerated examples to make a point.

Clearly you can't afford the quantities you need to test all this stuff at the same time (not to mention the fact that you probably couldn't find 200,000 good names in your market). Let's make this more realistic and start with looking for "direction" rather than predictability: two offers, two lists, and two letters. For now, forget the postcards, they never work as well as a letter. A real test grid you can do quite easily is shown in Table 3.

Table 3

Test Cell	Creative	List	Offer	Quantity
i	Letter 1	a	A	3,000 Test All
ii	"	"	B	3,000 Test Offer
iii	"	b	A	3,000 Test List
iv	"	b	B	2,000 Retest Offer
v	Letter 2	a	A	3,000 Test Creative
				14,000 Total

Let's up our budget to $12,000 (Table 4), so we can probably mail 3,000 pieces for each cell. We don't really need cell iv, but 5,000 is the minimum on most lists—so what the heck, let's use those extra 2,000 names to get another read on Offer B.

Table 4

Test Cell	Responses	Response %	Conversions To Sale	Conversions as % of total mailed
i	6	0.2%	2	0.067%
ii	7	0.23%	1	0.033%
iii	8	0.27%	2	0.067%
iv	4	0.2%	1	0.05% (2,000 mailed)
v	10	0.33%	3	0.1%
	35	0.25%	9	0.064%

This would be good. If all nine sales are incremental sales, you would have made about $60,000 in immediate revenue that you wouldn't have made otherwise. It would have cost you $12,000 plus your time, which we'll say was 50 hours ($5,000), so your profit is a little over $40,000. Not bad.

And you learned some important things: List b is probably better, Offer A is probably better, and Letter 2 is better. Can we quantify how much better when we put them all together? Sure, but remember we don't have enough results to know definitely, at least not yet.

In our little test, Letter 2, based just on conversions, is 50 percent better than Letter 1. But it also gave us 67 percent more responses. Conversions are a lot more important than responses, but you're going to start relationship efforts with those nonconverting responders. In cell i, Letter 1 gave you four of those, and in cell v, Letter 2 gave you seven of them. It's more likely that one of those seven non-converting responders will eventually buy or refer a buyer to you, so we can say that Letter 2 is more than 50 percent better than Letter 1.

Offers? It's probably a tie in this example, but I'd go with that extra sale in cell i for now. Let's say Offer A is 10 percent better than Offer B. Lists? b looks like a slight winner, say 10 percent better. Remember, we're just looking for direction at this point.

Table 5 shows what our next mailing might look like, with the combination of best elements working together as our control:

Table 5

Test Cell	Creative	List	Offer	Quantity
i	Letter 2	b	A	10,000 Control
ii	"	"	C	3,000 Test Offer
iii	"	c	A	3,000 Test List
iv	Letter 3	c	A	3,000 Test Creative

And the results might come in as shown in Table 6.

Table 6

Test Cell	Responses	Response %	Conversions To Sale	Conversions as % of total mailed
i	30	0.3%	10	0.1%
ii	11	0.367%	4	0.133%
iii	3	0.1%	0	0%
iv	15	0.5%	5	0.167%
	59	0.31	19	0.1%

I think the 19 sales here might be realistic. Now you'll roll out with Letter 3, Offer C, and stick with List b, testing new elements every time out.

The whole idea here is to test small and roll out when you have an indication, a direction, that one way is the better way. Stay cautious, track results and conversions, and always bet on winners.

Remember, the purpose of testing is to understand how much money you can spend to make a sale, and you get that from your DM allowable. If I were a real estate agent, I'd spend as much as I could afford to make sure my DM efforts start off with a first-class bang. Why? Well, one additional sale can mean an average of $6,600, so I'm not going to worry too much about improvements to my DM program that cost me a few hundred dollars.

Mail order math works in any medium. I use the mail because it's usually the most efficient medium. But you can test print ads and radio commercials, too. The principles are exactly the same. Find your DM allowable, test, track, and roll out with winning elements. And remember, you'll be investing, not spending.

TOOLS:DM Math

First figure out your DM allowable. Use the following formula:

Revenue – (Costs + cost of time) = DM allowable

Once you start testing your DM pieces, you'll need to keep track of how they're doing for you. Use these test grids to help keep track (see Chapter 3 for some guidelines on testing).

Test Cell	Creative	List	Offer

Test Cell	Responses	Response %	Conversions to Sale	Conversions as % of total mailed

Remember, DM math works for any medium—mail, print (magazine or newspaper), radio, or television.

The Successful Real Estate Marketer

Imagine this scenario: You have to move to Florida, and you haven't sold your apartment in New York yet. You also need to move your office and your staff. How much time do you have? About a month. Oh yes, you also have three speaking engagements in Istanbul, Turkey during that month.

That was my story in 2004. My mom was very ill, and I had to be close to her. My first challenge was finding a real estate agent. A friend mentioned a national company with an office in Miami, so I called and set up an appointment to fly down to look at some apartments.

My New York apartment was already under contract, and the buyers wanted to close in a month. I wasn't sure where I wanted to live in South Florida, but it had to be close to Mom's apartment in Miami Beach. I'd described what kind of apartment I needed to the

Miami agent and told her about my mom, and I was excited about seeing what she would recommend.

Talk about a letdown. She showed me places that were nothing like I'd described, including the near-my-mom requirement. I'm what they call geographically challenged, so it was a real disappointment to learn that the agent wasn't at all familiar with the Miami area. (Apparently she'd been in the business only a few months.) We wasted a lot of time looking at places I'd never buy. But I learned a lot, including the following:

1. The first thing a successful marketer does is *homework*. My first agent might have e-mailed me the listings the week before my visit and then organized the showings to make the best use of my time (and hers). Organizing the listings by address would have helped me zero in the neighborhood I liked best. A map would have helped me to understand our search.

   The agent who ultimately found my apartment for me did do her homework, and narrowed my search down to three buildings. She e-mailed me photos of one apartment when I was in Istanbul, and I sent her the money for the deposit. I knew she understood what I was looking for, and that really helped me through the process.

2. I'll bet that most great agents think of their clients as friends, because they want to keep them for a long time, and a mentality of "helping" your friends almost certainly works better than "selling" them.

   I bought my apartment in Florida without even seeing it in person, because I was in Istanbul at the time. Of course, I had no idea how I was going to manage the application for the mortgage and all the paperwork that goes with it. My Realtor told me about a mortgage agent at Bank of America, and I called him immediately.

   Peter Calia worked wonders to make my purchase possible. Recognizing my extreme aversion to paperwork, he took matters into his own hands and filled out the paperwork with me on the telephone. That was a massive relief.

   He then followed up regularly to keep me up to speed on the status of the loan. He gave the lawyers and my Realtor the news that a representative from his bank would attend the closing, and referred me to a building inspector who went over the apartment carefully—a very good idea, because it resulted in the seller allowing me credit on the sale price for minor repairs.

The whole process was seamless and effortless (for me), and I walked away with a positive feeling about Peter and the Bank of America. I figured that was the end of my dealing with him. But it wasn't.

Soon after I moved in, I began receiving Peter's monthly newsletter, "The Calia Chronicle." It is a motivational newsletter with nice stories, lists of weekly events for the month, and a P.S. reminding readers that if they know anyone who needs a mortgage, they might think of referring him. Naturally all his contact information was right there.

I was so impressed with Peter that I thought I'd ask him about his success secrets. Here's what he told me:

I started as a music teacher then worked as an assistant with a mortgage broker in a Publix supermarket. Maybe that hands-on experience taught me never to get comfortable, and I never really am.

I'm always marketing, because I never know when the economy might change. So I work like a dog. I keep in touch with clients with my newsletter "The Calia Chronicle" and with title companies and Realtors with my other newsletter called "Fetch."

Some of the things I do to be successful are: (1) I have a training class to help others learn how to juggle all of our priorities; (2) I have a marketing plan, and I make sure I meet it; (3) I break down the marketing plan so I have my goals each week; (4) I work constantly on new business, and try to capture every Realtor and then deliver the best service for that person. The way I do that is to get their work done for them before they ask; then I call and find out what they need from me for the closing. It is interesting that I have never even met 80 percent of the Realtors I work with.

Sixty percent of my business is from customer referrals, really 60 percent (15) of 25 loans each month.

Time management is essential. From nine to four I catch up on everything I'm working on, and then on Saturday I'm in the office from eight to eleven doing my entrepreneurial duties, and building the business. It is quiet, and I can think.

Successful marketer Peter Calia keeps in touch with clients using his newsletters "The Calia Chronicle" and "Fetch."

I have a "Calia Home Team" approach to my business, and we work to keep the pipeline full all the time. I'm in the top 5 percent of the country, and this year the bank sent us to Maui as a reward for our efforts.

3. I've noticed that great agents brand themselves, and that the brands reflect their personalities and, sometimes, the company's personality.

A brand can be a large company brand, like Met Life — you think of Snoopy selling insurance.

In the case of Realtors®, there are large ones like ReMax and Century 21, and within those brands there are some agents who stand out; they've either developed a niche in the marketplace or they've become known for some unique way they have of doing business.

When I think of this "brand" approach, I always think of my cousins, Mitch and Judy Milstein, known as the Super Team (mentioned in Chapter 8). Their tag-line is "Sell every time with Judy and Mitch Milstein," and they have their Super Team capes flying in some of their ads.

Their brand imagery works because Judy is very funny; the cartoon brings that humor across to their prospects.

Another brand image came across to me when I read in our local paper that Denise Rubin has been named Florida's Best Realtor® for the last two years, and is among Coldwell Banker's top 0.5 percent of agents worldwide.

I called her for an appointment, and her assistant set it up immediately. When I met with Denise, a very attractive lady, I asked about her success.

She told me that many owners try to sell their own properties nowadays, and she believes that's a mistake because they'd almost certainly get a higher price if they used a broker. Denise's value to her clients, aside from her charm, is in her network and her marketing skills. She's easy to talk to and rarely talks about her success, although there are many large plaques and trophies throughout her office.

I think her success stems from her quiet elegance and her wonderful talent of listening attentively. Good listening has to be high on every Realtor's success scale. She also followed up with a handwritten note.

4. Develop great people in your office, and they'll help you grow.

That is what happens all the time with Steven James, Senior Executive Vice President and Director of Sales for Prudential Douglas Elliman in New York City.

I called to ask about interviewing him for this book, and he graciously said yes. He told me that real estate is different these days because . . .

Some consumers and agents are stuck in the traditional mode of moving properties via a newspaper advertisement. Now, everything has changed because of the Internet.

In fact, I have one broker who is extraordinary, but her sales have been dropping. She was locked into the old way of doing business, and yet she's a specialist in her area of New York. Many brokers were coming into her area and taking away her market share. The reason was that she didn't have a cell phone. Also, we realized she needed to market in new ways on the Internet, though she didn't really use the computer. Our task was to help her to modify her way of doing business so she could compete.

The big change in the real estate industry in New York City is that many younger sales agencies are moving in, and they have strong professional credentials.

What kind of credentials, I asked?

Well, many have law school degrees and have practiced law for a few years; others are doctors and other people with substantial educational backgrounds. They found the workplace incredibly boring. They looked for something more fun and entrepreneurial, and, of course, in recent years real estate has been very lucrative.

Many times the lawyers don't do very well, because they don't have the salesmanship. This business is all about relating well to people and building relationships.

Our approach is we work in teams, and there are 500 people in this office and seven or eight teams. We usually have three star brokers who work with five other people and train them.

Do they do direct marketing together?

No, they design their own mailings and handle response rates and analysis. One woman used to be a marketing director for a large oil company, and she did a mailing of 10,000 pieces and received one response, which led to a property purchase. That was great, because you want your mailings to lead back to a deal.

We considered centralizing the marketing function, but our people are independent contractors and they want to do their own thing. Besides, if the company does the mailing, who gets the lead?

We used to get calls when people were looking to buy or sell multimillion dollar apartments. Those people don't call very often now, because they don't want to give you their name and telephone number. They say, "I don't want to tell you, because I'm not sure I want to work with you yet."

The calls that come in are usually for small apartments, like studios. The agents usually don't care that much about them and that is a mistake . . . because in reality, we should be working with people from cradle to grave.

My takeaway from Steven James is that he grows his people. He told me several times how wonderful his staff is, how they're adapting to the Internet. Steven James is truly a leader; he motivates his staff and is an excellent teacher for his group at Prudential Douglas Elliman.

5. Make a plan and stick to it. Don't file it away.

This is sound advice, and it comes from P. J. Martin Smith, Senior Vice President of Marketing for ERA Real Estate, a franchise company with offices worldwide. They have over 1,200 franchises domestically, more internationally, and over 38,000 real estate agents. They offer a variety of tools for their member franchises, including direct marketing tools. They help them to focus on the market, the purpose of the mailings (listings, referrals, capturing a specific demographic, etc.). They have a Direct Marketing Resource Center that takes their people through the entire process. The Resource Center also helps them to understand how they need to invest in themselves; perhaps one percent of their commissions go into marketing their businesses.

Ms. Smith told me that many agents forget to prospect when they're closing a deal. She encourages her agents to make a plan, figure out exactly how to invest their money, and commit to a dollar amount and a time frame . . . then do it. Also, she tells her agents to remember to measure the results of their marketing investments.

She also mentioned that she emphasizes keeping in touch with clients, keeping their lists up-to-date (by processing through the Change of Address file), and using all the tech tools to help keep in touch with buyers and sellers.

P. J. Martin Smith has over 30 years experience in the real estate business and is a true pro.

6. Create your own niche and customers will make a path to your door.

I met Roslyn Ceresne, an agent with Keyes Realty in Boca Raton, Florida, through a client, and she was interested in finding some new ideas for using direct marketing to build her business. So she came to visit Mason & Geller's marina office.

I asked her a lot of questions, and she enthusiastically shared with me her years of experience.

Roz's strength is in her knowledge of high-end waterfront property in Boca Raton. She works on getting those listings, and then she offers these special properties to people overseas.

First, she sells the area through ads in England, Belgium, Switzerland, or Germany. The ads run in the real estate sections of local business newspapers and in publications like the *Financial Times*.

She runs the same ad for about a year, describing the waterfront area, the golf course, the lovely blue water, the balmy evenings. Her headline reads: "Considering a vacation home?" Then, if enough people respond from that country, she books a flight and does a presentation there. At this writing, this works in her favor, because the Euro is doing well against the U.S. dollar. There's a lot of value here for our European neighbors.

When she meets with prospects, she doesn't talk about real estate. Instead, she talks about you, your family, politics, how many times a year you vacation. Then she tells potential buyers about the good schools and doctors in the area.

She also develops an A list, B list, and C list for her buyers. They always want to see her A list. This immediately positions the property. Nobody wants to see the C list.

Roz builds friendships with buyers and sellers and follows up with them (I know because she's one of the few agents I've interviewed who followed up with me). As you'd expect, she gets a lot of referrals. When she meets new prospects, she asks them how they bought their last homes. That's important, because she believes that people repeat their patterns.

I asked Roz about her company's brand and its importance. Her immediate response was that people buy the agent and what the agent will do for them. They don't buy the company. That's easy to understand when you're dealing with this star from Keyes Realty!

7. Successful marketers do unique things during the sale to make it happen, and afterward to be remembered.

Most of the people I spoke to said they often send "thank you" gifts after the sale. That is always a nice touch, because it means you'll be remembered fondly.

The best "thank you" gift I've heard about is BizBox, so I called and spoke to the owner of the company about his products, and this is what he told me.

The products are personalized moving boxes that agents give to their clients as appreciation gifts. The boxes are customized with the agent's name, contact information, and logo and photo, and they come in sets of 13, 23, or 36; they are shipped directly to the client. They are packaged in a big master box.

Agents who have used them have had a positive response, and 70 percent of them come back and order them again.

It works as a great idea for solidifying the business for future referrals, and as the people move out of their house, they see the agent's name and information on the boxes. It is also cost-efficient; the most expensive set of boxes is under $100.

The president of BizBox, Chad Armbruster, then told me the following story:

One of our agents went on a listing appointment and brought some of the boxes with him. When he walked up to the house, a neighbor saw the boxes and said they were getting ready to list their house, too. If we list with you, she asked, do we get the boxes also? The agent wrote up both listings that afternoon.

The boxes are used and kept after the move because they are high quality. On average clients receive 25 boxes. You are not trying to provide all of their moving needs, because they will probably use 50 to 100. You are just trying to help out by helping them to begin the moving process. People keep the boxes, because they're white and easy to locate after the move.

There are also tape and inserts available, and usually top producers give those as well.

You'll find the company at www.bizboxinc.com.

8. If you're an independent contractor, you are probably already an entrepreneurial type of person, and that means

Whether people are moving in or out of a house, the agent's name stands out on a BizBox.

you know your own strengths and weaknesses. So you know when to get help when you need it.

The professionals I talked to in the course of writing this book have solid support staff. Judy and Mitch Milstein support each other—she does the upfront relationship building, and he backs her up, getting the paperwork together, working on the marketing plans, and doing all the follow-up work in the office.

When I visited Denise Rubin's office in Aventura, Florida, I noticed people at the front desk posting her new MLS listings. Her son came in to visit, and he was showing some properties also. They were all working together to make the business even bigger than it already is.

Bob and Judy Mori in Connecticut also work as a team. He handles the listings, e-mail, and internet strategy. Judy shows the properties and is familiar with all of them.

Teamwork builds on the strengths of the group. At a RAMB Conference (REALTOR Association of Greater Miami & the Beaches), I sat next to a Realtor who told me he does it all, and "not that well," he admitted.

A few years back, we worked with a client who sold advertising space in huge directories and online for manufacturers. They'd been in the business for many years, and their business was gravitating from the books to the Internet. Their sales force resisted the change, though competitors were taking over their market share. Since their people were independent contractors, the company had little control over how they did their business. They tried to influence them and cajole them, but they were late adapters to the new technologies, and many of them lost out, leaving the company after investing many years in it. The point I want to make to you is that even if you don't know how to use a computer, a PDA, or even a cell phone—learn, or get someone to help you.

Successful marketers in real estate have to move with the times. One study mentioned that 80 percent of buyers are online, looking at properties. You want to be where the buyers will notice you, call, and purchase their next homes from you and your associates.

Rules and Tools for the Successful Marketer

✓ Do your homework; find out about the neighborhoods you are showing. This also includes organizing the showings, and your time. Keep a planner (or use a PDA). Organize your office and your car. Having a neat, clean appearance makes a good impression.

✓ Think of clients as friends, and build long-term relationships with them.

✓ Brand yourself or your company to reflect a personality. What image do you want to convey to prospects and clients?

✓ Develop your staff to be true professionals by adapting to the latest technology and always learning; attend seminars and training classes.

✓ Plan, Plan, and Plan some more. (See Chapter 9 for a DM plan.)

✓ Develop a niche for yourself, whether it be selling farm properties or being the "neighborhood" agent.

✓ Do unique things to make the sale happen for which you'll be remembered later. Send a thank-you gift and remember to promote loyalty and referrals.

✓ Get help if you need it.

New Creative Approaches

In direct marketing, the word *creative* refers to the words and images we use to communicate with customers and prospects — and it is an awful word for what we do.

We're not creative, we sell. We do exactly what the old door-to-door salesman, like the Fuller Brush Man, used to do, only we do it to hundreds, thousands, millions of people at the same time. The door-to-door salesman (and they were pretty much all men) dressed neatly (image) and spoke politely and clearly (like writing copy). He talked about his product, of course, but always in terms of what it would do for the prospect. And he made a unique, time-limited offer.

That's what we do.

Selling doesn't mean we're always hawking at our customers to buy something. "Selling" in the direct marketing sense means building a long-term relationship, and we might sell something right now or in the future, or both. A direct marketing relationship is always mutually beneficial, a win-win situation.

One of the problems is that *creative* has a different ring to it than *selling*. For one thing, creative sounds cool, glamorous. Everyone wants to be thought of as creative.

Creative also sounds easy. Selling is hard. Guess which appeals to most people?

The great Rosser Reeves, a 1950s ad man, once wrote that "Advertising is the art of getting a Unique Selling Proposition into the heads of the most people at the lowest possible cost."

We direct marketers have changed that slightly: "Direct marketing is the art and science of getting the right offer into the right hands at the right time . . . at the lowest possible cost."

Another great ad man, Claude Hopkins, invented "Scientific Advertising" and wrote a book about it back in the 1920s. It's still considered one of the top four or five books on advertising. He wrote: "The good salesman does not merely cry a name. He doesn't say, *Buy my article*. He pictures the customer's side of his service until the natural result is to buy. A brush maker has some 2,000 canvassers who sell brushes from house to house. He is enormously successful in a line that would seem very difficult. And it would be if his men asked the housewives to buy. But they don't. They go to the door and say, *I was sent here to give you a brush. I have samples here and I want you to take your choice*. The housewife is all smiles and attention. In picking out one brush she sees several she wants. She is also anxious to reciprocate for the gift. So the salesman gets an order.

> You can read Claude Hopkins's entire book on line at http://www.successprofessor.com/scientific_advertising/. I recommend it.

Unfortunately, the concept "creative" has been appropriated by art directors and copywriters, mostly in advertising agencies; it's almost as if putting words and pictures together has become a religion, and they're the high priests. That's all nonsense, of course. The most creative people in direct marketing are the strategists, planners, list planners, the people who come up with offers, database whizzes, and the kind of people who offered brushes door to door.

They're like my dad, a jewelry manufacturer in New York City, who used to say, "Do something the other guy isn't doing." It takes curiosity and *chutzpah*—nerve—to do that, and it can't happen until you do your homework and create a plan. (See Chapter 9; in the meantime, remember the adage, *If you fail to plan, you're planning to fail.*) The discipline of writing out everything you want to do, what's available to help you do it, and how you intend to actually do it will help your big idea sprout and grow.

Another problem with "creative" is that it's enormously distracting for people who should know better. I've lost count of how many times I've been in senior level meetings at huge corporations, watching people get so stuck in huge debates about creative matters that they lose track of the really important things like developing a reasonable objective, testing, timing, fine tuning the offer, understanding the target audience, working the numbers, and figuring out the details of response management. *Planning*, in other words.

Once your plan is down on paper and everyone understands it, then you can start working on the *relevant* tactical approaches and creative ideas that will drive your strategy.

The best way to get started is to **be curious**. Curious people are always wondering about things the rest of us don't even think about. The 3M company in Minnesota is filled with curious people. The company makes something like 67,000 products—you'd think that would be enough, but it isn't, because all those curious people are always coming up with something new. Post-it™ Notes, for instance. One of 3M's employees was curious about a new temporary glue. What use could it possibly be? Then one evening he was at choir practice, flipping from this hymn to that hymn and losing his place—and it hit him: maybe that glue on a small piece of paper. The next thing you know, 3M had a wonderful new product.

Curious people just naturally think of ways **to improve things**, and they don't pay much attention to the rut everyone else is stuck in. One of my favorite examples was in an old TV show called "The Tycoon," starring Walter Brennan. He was the tycoon, and he'd brought some of his executives to a company he was thinking of buying. One of the young executives disappeared while the rest of them toured the plant, went over the books, and did all the usual things executives do. After a while Brennan got mad about the young fellow who'd just disappeared; he was going to fire him when the guy finally showed up. "Where have you been?" demanded Brennan. The young man had been observing the assembly line, and he'd noticed that the way the product came off the line was far too slow. He'd figured out that if they put a left-handed worker at the end of the line, the worker could complete the end of the line more efficiently. He was curious, watched the way things worked, and came up with a great, simple, doable idea that never would have occurred to anyone else.

I thought of that as I was reading the *New York Post* a while back. A big-time property developer in New York had thrown a huge party for new owners and prospects.

> *The other day, Orin Wilf, the developer of 170 East End Avenue, a family-friendly building, sponsored an invitation-only concert in Carl Schurz Park with Laurie Berkner and her band, plus carnival games, face painting and cotton candy. Anyone with a young child knows Berkner is No. 1 with the kiddies set.*

> — *New York Post,* Wednesday, June 22, 2006

This developer was aiming their promotion party at their target market—couples with children. They also wanted to have those families talk about the building to their friends.

Another developer, Zeckendorf, had a concert at Lincoln Center, and it was memorable for everyone who attended, which was by invitation only. Usually in New York, apartments are on and off the market so quickly that the owners don't have to promote vacancies at all. But these apartments start at $1,000,000 and go way up from there. That market is slowing, so creatively curious developers decided to see what would happen if they tried events to build relationships with their upscale prospects.

Will it sell apartments? I don't know. Did the developer figure out the cost of the party, and how many units he'd have to sell to break even on the event? Did he think of alternate ways to bring in prospects? I have a sneaking suspicion that the concert/party idea does have legs. It's designed to get the right people together, and it's a creative idea, something the other guy isn't doing.

Events, the right events, can work wonders. Maroone, a big time car dealer in South Florida, rents the Dolphins football stadium for special sale events. Maybe you can test an event with a much more modest investment; for example:

- A free seminar for first-time home buyers that will help them figure out what kind of home they can afford. You'll tell them how to learn the hidden costs of home ownership, like closing costs, taxes, assessments, maintenance, lawn upkeep, and so on. You don't even need to pay for a room or an ad in the paper if you put together an outline for your seminar and ask the local Rotary Club, Chamber of Commerce, or Kiwanis Club to sponsor the event for their members. They can mention it in their newsletter and on their website (as well as get word of mouth circulating.) Organizations like good speakers who focus on providing useful information, in this case helping people to buy their first home with more confidence that they're getting the right kind of deal.
- Consider trying an event at your next Open House. Last weekend, I went to several Open Houses in my area. The first house I visited was very nice, but the agent there was selling at me the whole time, so I barely had time to think about the house. He also didn't ask me to sign the guest book, so he could database my information. If he had, he might have remembered that I want a place with three bedrooms and three baths and then, when he had one, he could have called me. He was too busy selling, rather than marketing. Short term—sell this house; instead of long term—sell lots of houses. Maybe it works for him, but I'm pretty sure he missed a golden opportunity. I would have had a stack of small (inexpensive) wrapped gifts near the signup book with a stand-up sign offering a "thank you gift" for giving us your name and information. I would have asked a local caterer to bring over some finger food, and I would have mentioned it in the ad. Or I would have offered a package of gift certificates from neighborhood restaurants, dry cleaners, stationery stores. Will any of this work? Over time, yes.

- Try becoming **the real estate authority** in your market. One way is to write about what you know best, real estate. You can do this by creating "keeper" brochures such as *Ten Important Things to Consider before You Buy Your New Home.* Offer to write a column in a local newspaper, even a weekly or Penny Saver, with genuinely helpful information about real estate. People will begin to think of you as the reliable authority.
- You might also start doing regular surveys, just four or five questions, tabulating the results, and publishing them in your own newsletter or brochure. People love reading that kind of stuff.
- As you start to become known as an authority, you can begin speaking at the local marketing counsel or real estate association. Let the local press know what you're going to talk about and when. (Make sure it's something they'll want to cover — if you're not sure what that is, ask them.) Public speaking means that many more people know about you — especially when your speeches are mentioned in the press — and that helps your business in many unexpected and wonderful ways.

Customer behavior is the most fascinating part of marketing; it's always a great idea to get curious about understanding it and managing it.

- Keep an eye on people who register on your website and track what kinds of homes they look at (price, neighborhood, size, amenities, etc.); alert them the instant you have something that you know will interest them. This is inexpensive precision database marketing of the highest order.
- Test your assumptions about what people really want from you. You might be surprised. I certainly was when I read the *Harvard Business Review* of June, 2006, and came across this in an article titled *"More Isn't Always Better"*:

Marketers assume that the more choices you offer, the more likely customers will be able to find just the right thing. They assume, for instance, that offering 50 styles of jeans instead of two increases the chances that the shoppers will find a pair they really like. Nevertheless, research now shows that there can be too much choice; when there is, consumers are less likely to buy anything at all, and if they do buy, they are less satisfied with their selection.

From *"More Isn't Always Better,"* by Barry Schwartz

That reminded me of Keyes Realty's Roz Ceresne, who simplifies choices for her buyers with three lists: A, B, and C. There are two properties on each list, with the best on A and the worst on C. Prospects usually ask for the B list first and the A list second. She says that almost nobody asks to look at the C list. Narrowing choices could help your prospects decide on a new home and be happy about their decision.

- Stay in touch with your prospects (and clients who've bought) with an e-mail newsletter with featured listings and tips on the many and varied aspects of buying a new home, moving, and selling an existing property. Electronic newsletters are terrific and inexpensive relationship builders, especially when you allow your personality to shine through.
- You can get your name out there by sponsoring a Little League team and/or good neighbor events like Clean Up the Park Day, sponsored by you. You can sponsor a gift package for graduating high school kids whose parents might be getting ready to move.
- Consider doing ads, direct mail, a website with a unique brand. In two ads that I wrote and Pepper Huff designed, we created two new company names for realties. The first one is Welcome Homes, and the second one is Rembrandt Properties, "The Fine Art of Real Estate."

With both of these brands, you can have a lot of fun with a play on words. With Welcome Homes, you can give all your homeowners the mat, and use the logo in everything . . . and it sounds warm and fuzzy too.

Welcome to 725 Eleventh Avenue, Hollywood Florida

This Spanish style cottage is situated in the lovely lakes section of Hollywood. You can tell that a true horticulturist designed the landscaping as you enter under a bower of Hibiscus flowers.

The living room looks out on the back tiled terrace that has a lovely overhang that shades you from the Florda sun. The new state of the art kitchen leads out into the dining room that has a "secret" hallway to an extra bedroom and den area. Two full bedrooms and bathrooms are on the opposite side of the home, which has been newly recreated with tile, air conditioning, roof and magnificent crown moldings.

It is a home in move-in condition and grounds you will enjoy for years to come. Offered at $599,000.

Call Lois Geller at: 646-723-3231, and ask Her for your Free copy of *"10 Insider Secrets To Buying Your New Home"*...Now.

WELCOME ™ HOMES

646.123.1234 • www.welcomehomes.com • lois@welcomehome.com
123 Marina Drive Suite 201 • Hollywood, FL 12345-1234

This "Welcome" ad appears to be inviting you in the front door.

725 ELEVENTH AVENUE · HOLLYWOOD, FL

This Spanish style cottage is situated in the lovely lakes section of Hollywood. You can tell that a true horticulturist designed the landscaping as you enter under a bower of Hibiscus flowers.

The living room looks out on the back tiled terrace that has a lovely overhang that shades you from the Florda sun. The new state of the art kitchen leads out into the dining room that has a "secret" hallway to an extra bedroom and den area. Two full bedrooms and bathrooms are on the opposite side of the home, which has been newly recreated with tile, air conditioning, roof and magnificent crown moldings.

It is a home in move-in condition and grounds you will enjoy for years to come.

It is a Rembrandt property...awaiting the right family to frame its future. Offered at $599,000. **Call Lois Geller at:** **646-723-3231**, and ask Her for your Free copy of *"10 Insider Secrets To Buying Your New Home"*...Now.

REMBRANDT PROPERTIES
THE FINE ART OF REAL ESTATE

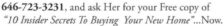

646.123.1234 • www.rembrandtrealty.com • lois@rembrandtrealty.com
123 Marina Drive Suite 201 • Hollywood, FL 12345-1234

Rembrandt Properties, the Fine Art of Real Estate, is working to position the brand as "upscale."

Rembrandt Properties can be used to paint a picture of your next wonderful home, investment property, or vacation abode. Rembrandt's image is elegant and sounds up-scale, so I had some fun writing the copy.

Take a look at the ads, and let me know what you think by faxing or e-mailing me (see the last page of this book for my information . . . "I'd Like To Hear From You").

There are a limitless number of creative approaches to building your business if you're curious, want to improve your business, and can keep things simple. You know that your next idea will probably be much better than a postcard with a photo of a property. Everyone does that, and you want to *do what the other guy isn't doing.* You know, of course, that if you continue to do what you've always done, you'll get what you have always gotten. Try new creative approaches, keep track of what happens, and go forth and conquer!

And please, e-mail me, call, or write—I want to know how you're doing.

Lois K. Geller

I'd Like to Hear from You

Dear Lois,

I've just finished reading *Sold! Direct Marketing for the Real Estate Pro.*

Can you direct me to the following resources in my area– computer service bureau, letter shop, etc?

_____

_____

_____

Can you send me more information about

_____

_____

_____

I'd like some feedback on a direct marketing campaign I'm planning. My plans include–

_____

_____

_____

_____

(If needed, attach a separate sheet.)

Please add me to your mailing list for all your free communications–

Name _____

Title _____

Company _____

Street _____

City _____ State _____ Zip _____

E-mail _____

Contact me at–
Lois K. Geller
Mason and Geller Direct
1400 Marina Drive
Hollywood, FL 33019
Tel– 646-723-3230
Fax– 954-456-2877
E-mail: loisgeller@masongeller.com

Glossary of Direct Marketing Terms

Address Correction Requested–When this phrase is printed on the upper left-hand corner of the direct mail envelope, it is telling the post office to provide a new address if the person no longer lives at the address indicated. There is a charge for this service and it is a good way to update your mailing list.

banner ad–This is an advertisement placed on a website either above, below, or on the sides of the website's main content and is linked to the advertiser's own website.

benefits–All the reasons a person should buy a product so it will enhance his or her personal life, career, well-being.

bleed–This term refers to reproducing an illustration or photograph so that is covers the entire page, leaving no margin. An ad that runs off one, two, three, or four sides of the page is called a bleed ad; most publications charge more for its use, as the ad is larger than if it had a margin around it.

brochure–A flyer, broadside, or bound printed piece included in your direct mail package. This piece usually highlights a product and offer, and should include all the benefits of the product.

bulk mail–Large quantities of direct mail (packages, catalogs, self-mailers) that are sorted before going to the post office. Bulk mail allows the mailer to qualify for discounts.

Cheshire label–A mailing label that is imprinted by the computer and cut (by a Cheshire machine) into individual labels on a long sheet. They are then glued to the direct mail packages by machine at the letter shop. Cheshire labels are less expensive than pressure-sensitive labels, which you can peel off and stick onto envelopes.

cleaning–List cleaning refers to keeping the list as up-to-date as possible by eliminating duplicate names and incorporating changes of address.

click–The action of a user pressing the mouse button, generally to cause an action on a computer.

compiled list–A list of names and addresses that are created specifically to be used by direct marketers. The names are usually taken from directories, census information, and registration files. Compiled lists have specific target markets—for instance, all pediatricians, school principals, or car owners.

comp layout–This phrase is short for comprehensive layout. A comprehensive layout can be done for a whole direct mail package, a catalog, or an advertisement. It shows the placement of the photographs and type, in correct proportions, and allows changes to be made before costly separations and plates are made.

computer service bureau–A service that provides a variety of mailing services, such as list maintenance, merge/purge, list rental, subscription fulfillment, and database manipulation. Since this is the only type of work computer service bureaus do, they can usually do it more economically than a company could do in-house.

creative–Sometimes a shortened form of "creative strategy," creative refers to the comprehensive layout of an advertisement, direct mail campaign, or catalog.

database–A database is a collection of information, stored in a computer, which can be readily accessed as needed. The type of information you might want to retrieve (besides basic name and address) includes your most recent clients, clients who have bought from you frequently, customers who have children, etc.

demographics–Statistics about clients that refer to external life patterns—such as age, sex, income level, education, or size of family.

FSI–Free-standing Insert, or an advertisement, booklet, catalog, or brochure that is inserted in a newspaper (usually the Sunday edition). The newspaper charges a fee for inserting an FSI, usually a cost per thousand.

hotline buyers– Customers who have recently purchased something or inquired about a service, usually in the last three months.

house file–An internal list that includes customer information. It can be formatted as a marketing database or a simple list of clients and transactions.

inquiry–Usually a request for information, it is sometimes a way for direct marketers to generate names of prospects they can convert to buyers. These inquiries then become leads for follow-up mailings or sales calls.

involvement device–Sometimes called an action device, the recipient is asked to check off "yes," "no," of "maybe" on the order form, or to peel off a stamp or sticker and move it from the mailing piece to the order form. It is a device used in direct marketing to get the prospect actively involved with a mailing.

Johnson Box–A graphic device used to highlight a particular message or offer in a sales letter of a direct mail package. It is placed above the salutation, and it used to be made of asterisks forming the box. Now it is sometimes printed to look as if it were hand-written.

key code–See source code.

layout–A sketch of what a marketing piece will look like after it is printed. It shows where the copy will be and where photographs or illustrations will appear, as well as the typefaces that will be used. Layouts can be shown at various phases of a particular job. A writer's roughs or the rough layout is usually a sketch of how the creative team envisions the piece. A finished layout is more detailed and may even include some photography in place. A comprehensive layout shows exactly how the finished piece will look. Sometimes layouts are produced on a computer and sometimes they are rendered by hand.

lettershop–Sometimes called a mailing house, this facility does all the preparation necessary to get direct mail into the post office and into the homes (or businesses) of recipients, including list and label preparation, personalization, as well as stuffing, addressing, collating, and sorting envelopes.

list–The names and addresses of individuals and businesses having a specific interest or purchase history. There are three kinds of lists: in-house, direct response, and compiled.

list broker–A specialist who researches appropriate lists for mailing, recommends lists to the mailer, gets the lists to the lettershop on time for the mailing, and following the mailing, does an evaluation of the lists' performance.

list manager–A person or company who works for the list owner and is responsible for marketing the list to list users and list brokers. The manager is also responsible for the maintenance of the list, all clearances necessary before the mail date, record keeping, and billing. The list manager may also be the list broker.

list rental–An agreement; frequently handled by a broker, between a list owner and a list user whereby the owner provides names and addresses to the mailer on a one-time basis. The mailer pays the owner at an agreed upon rate per thousand names. Most lists are delivered to the mailer's lettershop on a disk or Cheshire labels.

loyalty program–A program designed to make customers want to patronize a particular company more frequently than they may have. One of the most familiar loyalty programs is the frequent flyer plan.

merge/purge–A computer process that combines two or more lists to eliminate duplicates and undesirable names in order to provide the best list for a promotion.

offer–A unique promotion put to consumer prior to the consumer's consent to buy. A newspaper offer might be five daily issues for $2 ($1 off the newsstand price). The offer becomes a contract when the completed order form is returned to the vendor.

offer test–A test in a direct marketing promotion that varies a price or offer element. It is important in a direct marketing test to change only one portion of a package at a time, so that any differences in the response rate of the test package can be measured against the control.

opt-in e-mail–E-mail communication which only happens if the recipient has specifically requested it from the particular source.

opt-out–An option to unsubscribe from receiving e-mail solicitations from an online marketer, online magazine, or any other source. This area is becoming increasingly regulated and providing an opt-out hyperlink in any direct marketing email has become standard practice.

package–The sum of all components in a direct mail promotion (outer envelope, business reply envelope, letter, inserts, order form, lift letter, etc.).

response rate–The gross responses received from a direct marketing program as a percentage of the total number of direct mail pieces sent or contacts that were made with readers, radio listeners, or televisions viewers. A response can be either a purchase or an inquiry which can be converted to a purchase.

roll out–The mailing to a full list after a portion of that list has tested well.

seasonality–A pattern in a marketing program in which response shows variation with the changes of the season. Every product should be tested to see if there are certain months which will outperform others.

sectional center–Sometimes referred to as SCF (Sectional Center Facility), this is a U.S. Postal Service mail-handling distribution unit that serves a group of post offices whose ZIP codes all begin with the same first three digits.

self-mailer–A self-contained direct mail piece, usually including a reply form that is mailed without an envelope.

solo mailing–A mailing to promote a single product or service, which usually consists of a letter, a brochure, and a reply device enclosed in an outer envelope.

source code–A series of numbers or an alphanumeric code placed on an order form, coupon, or other response mechanism. Each offer has its own code so that marketers can determine and compare the responses.

space ad–An advertisement in a print medium such as a newspaper or magazine. This space is sold to advertisers on the basis of the size of the ad, the position of the ad, and the circulation of the publication.

test–The evaluation phase of a program where one or more elements of a program are introduced to a relatively small audience. All facets of a program are then evaluated and the most successful are rolled out to a larger audience. In a direct mail test, the elements usually tested are product, offer, list, and creative.

testimonial–Often used in direct marketing copy to add credibility to your promotion, a testimonial is a statement made by a customer who is satisfied with a product or service. This statement may be made by a public figure or any satisfied customer.

test panel–A sample group taken from a full list of people to test out a specific creative approach or a new offer.

Third Class–The U.S. Postal Service's designation for bulk mail, including direct mail packages and catalogs that weigh less than one pound. Special discounted rates are permitted if mailings meet certain presort requirements and quantity levels. A third-class permit is required.

website–A series of linked pages which might function in a variety of ways, such as an online store, an association with online resources, a service organization or a family of websites.

ZIP code–ZIP is an abbreviation for Zoning Improvement Plan, and is a way for the U.S. Postal Service to identify where a particular piece of mail is going. It was designed for easier sorting and dispatching, and was expanded from the original five-digit code to ZIP+4, nine digits in total.

ZIP code analysis–A way of analyzing how many orders come from particular ZIP codes, so that direct marketers can track their best and worst prospects geographically.

Resource Directory

Associations

National Association of REALTORS®
500 New Jersey Ave. NW
Washington, D.C. 20001-2020
(800) 874-6500
www.realtor.org

The National Association of REALTORS® is an essential resource for real estate agents, with more than 1.2 million members in the U.S. (and a presence in nearly 60 countries). Founded in 1908, the NAR provides its members with the education, training, resources, and tools necessary to build success. They have many resources available; here are just a few–

- *Technology, such as computers and software*
- *Marketing*
- *Insurance, many different types*
- *Finance, including credit cards and banking*
- *Industry publications, including REALTOR® magazine and a wide array of books and manuals*
- *Free listings on www.realtor.com*
- *Representation in government, for the purpose of the free enterprise system and the right to own real property*
- *Members of the NAR must subscribe to its Code of Ethics and Standards of Practice*

With all of their offerings, the NAR is an association that helps the real estate profession . . . and the real estate professional.

REALTOR® Association of Greater Miami and the Beaches
700 S. Royal Poinciana Blvd. Ste. 400
Miami, FL 33166
(305) 468-7000
www.miamire.com

The NAR *has many other state and local chapters; visit* www.realtor.org/directories/index.html *for more information.*

Client Gifts and Promotional Items

4-Imprint
101 Commerce Street
PO Box 320
Oshkosh, WI 54903-0320
(877) 446-7746
www.4imprint.com

BizBox, Inc.
Mr. Chad Armbruster
2717 SW Cannock Chase
Topeka, KS 66614
(877) 7BizBox
www.bizboxinc.com

Blooming Cookies
150 Ottley Drive
Atlanta, GA 30324
(800) 435-6877
www.bloomingcookies.com

Entertainment Publications
1414 E. Maple Road
Troy, MI 48083
(800) 672-3053
www.entertainment.com

Fruition Gifts
P.O. Box 2001
Jessup, MD 20794
(800) 481-3784
www.fruitiongifts.com

Contests, Promotions, and Sweepstakes

Ventura Associates
1040 Avenue of the Americas
New York, NY 10018
(212) 302-8277
www.sweepspros.com

Creative Services

Mason & Geller Direct Marketing
1400 Marina Drive
Hollywood, FL 33019
(646) 723-3230
www.masongeller.com

Digital Media

InmanStories
1480 64th Street, Suite 100
Emeryville, CA 94608
(510) 658-9292 ext 147
info@inmanstories.com
www.inmanstories.com

Direct Marketing Publications

Direct
P.O. Box 10756
Riverton, NJ 08076-0756
(888) 892-3613
www.primediabusiness.com

DM News
P.O. Box 2037
Skokie, IL 60076
(847) 588-0675
www.dmnews.com

Target Marketing
North American Publishing Co
1500 Spring Garden Street, Suite 1200
Philadelphia, PA 19130
(800) 777-8074
www.targetonline.com

Lois's "Creative Corner" column appears in Target Marketing *bi-monthly.*

Direct Marketing Training & Speeches

Lois K. Geller
1400 Marina Drive
Hollywood, FL 33019
(646) 723-3230
loisgeller@masongeller.com

List Brokers

Automated Resources Group International
135 Chestnut Ridge Road
Montvale, NJ 07645
(201) 391-1500
www.callargi.com

Direct Media
200 Pemberwick Road
Greenwich, CT 06830
(203) 532-1000
www.directmedia.com

Dunhill International List Co
621 NW 53rd Street, Ste. 200
Boca Raton, FL 33487-8239
(800) 386-4455
www.dunhills.com

Mortgage Lenders

Peter Calia
Mortgage Direct Lender
Bank of America
6505 Blue Lagoon Drive, Ste. 150
Miami, FL 33126
(305) 756-1880

Photography

Mr. Michael Shopenn
Michael Shopenn Photography
620 N. 34th Street #216
Seattle, WA 98103
(336) 558-8339
mshopenn@mac.com

Printers

DPI (Digital Printers International)
16200 NE 13th Avenue
North Miami Beach, FL 33162
(305) 948-2311
www.dpibizcards.com

Nahan Printing
Joan Smuda
7000 Saukview Drive
St. Cloud, MN 56302
(320) 251-7611
www.nahan.com

Real Estate Agents

Roslyn Ceresne
Keyes Company
405 Plaza Real; Boca Mizner
Boca Raton, FL 33432
(561) 391-9503
www.keyes.com/roslyn.ceresne

ERA Real Estate
One Campus Drive
Parsippany, NJ 07054
(800) 869-1260
www.era.com

Reba Miller
RP Miller & Associates
115 E 57th Street, Suite 1103
New York, NY 10022
(212) 980-4449
www.rpmillerassociates.com

Judy & Mitch Milstein
c/o Long & Foster Real Estate, Inc.
7719 Tuckerman Lane
Potomac, MD 20854
(301) 520-3694
www.superteamhomes.com

Steven James
Senior Executive VP & Director of Sales–Eastside
Prudential Douglas Elliman
575 Madison Avenue, 5th Floor
New York, NY 10022
(212) 891-7277
www.elliman.com

Bob & Judy Mori
Team Mori Real Estate
2242 Huntington Turnpike
Trumbull , CT 06611
(866) 385-0090
www.TeamMoriRealEstate.com

Denise Rubin
Coldwell Banker Real Estate
20803 Biscayne Blvd. #102
Aventura, FL 33180
(305) 459-5039
www.deniserubin.com

Simon Salloom
Coldwell Banker Real Estate
Brentwood Court
11611 San Vicente Boulevard
Los Angeles, CA 90049
(310) 442-1377
www.simonsalloom.com

Diane Silverman
Keller Williams Realty
120 Bloomingdale Road
White Plains, NY 10605
(914) 482-3445
www.dianesilverman.com

Sales Training

The Nierenberg Group
Ms. Andrea Nierenberg
420 E. 51st Street; Suite 12D
New York, NY 10022
(212) 980-0930
www.mybusinessrelationships.com

About the Author

Lois K. Geller is founder and president of Mason & Geller Direct, a full-service direct response agency. She was previously president of AC&R Direct, a Saatchi and Saatchi agency; Geller Direct, a TBWA subsidiary; J. Walter Thompson Direct; and Vickers and Benson Direct, in Toronto. Lois is the author of *Response! The Complete Guide to Profitable Direct Marketing* (revised 2002, and now published in nine languages); *Direct Marketing Techniques*, and *Customers For Keeps*. She has appeared on CNN, CBS, and the Jim Blasingame Show and speaks often at industry events and conferences. Her direct response articles appear regularly in *Direct Marketing Magazine, Today's Manager*, and *Selling Power;* her "Creative Corner" column is a monthly feature of *Target*

Marketing Magazine; and her "Direct Marketing Diva" column is featured in *Fortune On-Line.* Lois has been an adjunct professor at New York University, where she leads the Direct Marketing Lecture Series and was named Professor of the Year in 1999. In 1999 she won the Silver Apple Award for Lifetime Achievement in Direct Marketing and has received the Echo Award in direct marketing and many RSVP Awards in Canada. Lois Geller lives in Aventura, Florida, with offices in Hollywood, Florida. She can be reached at loisgeller@masongeller.com

Index

Access, Microsoft, 68
action devices, 31, 34, 38, 159
Address Correction Requested, 157
ads, space, 14, 97–109, 151–154, 157,
    161–162
advertising, direct response. *See* direct
    response advertising
advertising, general, 15–16
allowable, direct marketing, 16,
    125–126, 131
Altberg, Marla, 34
American Express, 9–10, 16
analyzing test results, 35, 36, 110.
    See also testing
Armbruster, Chad, 141–142
authority, establishing self as, 150

Babcock, Dolores Ryan, 42
background for campaign planning,
    114–115, 119
banner ads, 157. *See also* ads, space
behavior, customer, 150–151
benefits, 11–14, 157
BizBox, 141–142
bleed, 157
branding
    determining, 21–23, 78
    examples, 80–83, 137, 151–154
    importance, xv, 141
Brennan, Walter, 147–148
broadcast media, 110
brochures, 150, 157
brokers, list, 40–42, 46–47, 160
budgets, 15, 104–105, 117–118, 120
building relationships. *See* relationship
    building

Bulk Mail, 157
buyers, hotline, 47, 158

cable television, 110
Calia, Peter, 134–136
calls to action, 29, 74, 95, 97, 109
campaign plans. *See* planning
cards, list, 46–51
cells, test, 35–36, 126–132, 162
Century 21, 45, 78, 137
Ceresne, Roslyn, 17, 140–141, 151
checklists, planning, 119–121
Cheshire labels, 157
choices, customer, 150–151
cleaning, list, 47, 75, 158
clicks, 158
client needs, 134–135
codes, source, 19, 35, 111, 161
Coldwell Banker, 45, 58, 80, 137
commissions, 32–36, 124–125
compiled lists, 42–43, 158. *See also* lists
comprehensive layouts, 158
computer service bureaus, 158
Consumer Reports, 67
contact management systems, 68–69, 75
contingency plans, 118, 120
control, 34–35, 130–131
Corcoran, 78
costs, 15, 104–105, 117–118, 120
creative, direct mail, 77–95, 158
    branding, 80–83
    "do's," 93–95
    types, 83–92
creative approaches, 145–154
    examples and techniques, 149–154
    overview, 145–149

creative *versus* selling, 145–147
curiosity, 147–148
customer behavior, 150–151
customer choices, 150–151
customer retention programs, 33, 160
customer service, 133–136
customers, profiling and targeting,
       12–13, 23–24, 41–45, 51,
       79–80, 117

databases, 65–76
   marketing with, 44–45, 66–67, 71–76,
      93, 109
   overview, 65–67, 158
   tools, 67–70
demographics, 51, 66, 158
developing people, 137–139
DEW (Distant Early Warning) lines,
   29–30
Direct Magazine, 32
direct mail creative. *See* creative, direct
   mail
direct mail math. *See* math, direct mail
direct mail overview, 14–15, 77–80, 99
direct marketing, xv, 5–7, 9–11, 14–15,
   21, 146
direct marketing allowable, 16,
   125–126, 131
Direct Marketing Association (DMA),
   40, 46
direct response advertising, 97–111.
     See also specific types
   elements, 101–110
   overview, 97–101
direct response lists, 43. *See also* lists
DiSciullo, Henry, 44–45
discounts, 32
DM News, 32
Duncan, Karen, 61

early bird offers, 32
e-mail marketing, 63–64, 70, 75
ERA Real Estate, 139–140
estimates, 117–118, 120
events, 147–149, 151
experts, establishing as, 150

Financial Times, 17, 140
follow-ups, 74–75, 93
Ford, 116–117
40–40–20 rule, 31, 40
"free" offers, 30–32, 37
FSI's (Free-standing Inserts), 14, 105, 158

general advertising, 15–16
gifts, 45, 87, 141–142, 144
goal setting, 113, 135
grids, test, 126–132

Harvard Business Review, 150–151
Hertz, 79
homepages, 56
homework, 134, 144
Hopkins, Claude, 146
hotline buyers, 47, 158
house files, 41–43, 159
Huff, Pepper, 83, 87, 107–109, 151–154

Incentives Magazine, 32
incrementability, 123–126, 131
in-house lists, 41–44, 159
Inman, Brad, 61
Inman News, 61
inquiries. *See* responses
Internet paradox, 56
involvement devices, 31, 34, 38, 159

James, Steven, 137–139
Jeworski, Dwain, 32–33, 56–57, 71–76
Johnson Boxes, 159
just-in-time mailings, 83

Keller Williams Realty, 83
key codes, 19, 35, 111, 161
Kinney, Teresa King, 58
knowledge level, working from, 45

lagniappe, 27–31
Land's End, 58–59
layouts, 159
lead generation, 33, 36–37, 68, 71–72,
     97, 109–110. *See also* responses
lead status, 75

letters, 3, 16, 21, 77–78, 86–92
lettershops, 40, 46, 47, 159
list brokers, 40–42, 46–47, 160
list cards, 46–51
list cleaning, 47, 75, 158
list managers, 40, 160
list plans, 46, 51
list rentals, 46–47, 160
list selections, 46–51
lists, 39–51
   choosing, 43–51, 117
   overview, 39–42, 158, 160
   types, 42–43
loyalty programs, 33, 160

magazine ads, 14, 105. *See also* ads, space
mailing houses, 46, 47, 159
managers, list, 40, 160
Mason and Geller Direct, 4, 16, 54,
   78, 113
math, direct mail, 4, 123–132
   determining incrementability,
      123–126, 131
   test grids and response rates, 35–36,
      126–132, 162
McCormick, Mike, 63, 79
MCI, 33
measuring results, 6, 15–16, 18–21, 110
member-get-a-member offers, 33–34
merging/purging, 160
Miami Herald, 97
Microsoft, 68
Miller, Reba, 98–99
Milstein, Mitch and Judy, 101–102,
   137, 143
MLS (multiple listing service),
   69–70, 103
"More Isn't Always Better," 150–151
Mori, Bob, 33, 56–57, 143

National Association of Realtors, 70
NCOA (National Change of
   Address), 75
networking, 17
New York Post, 97–99, 148
New York Times, 103, 104

newsletters, 17–18, 54, 135–136, 151
newspaper ads, 14, 104–105. *See also*
   ads, space
niches, 140–141, 144

objectives, 115, 120
offers, direct marketing, 27–38
   examples, 36–37
   overview, xv–xvi, 12–13, 27–34, 39,
      74, 160
   testing, 18–21, 34–38, 160
offers, real estate, 12, 27, 29
open houses, 32, 87–88, 149
opt-in e-mails, 160
opt-outs, 161
outside lists. *See* lists

packages, 86, 161
people, developing, 137–139
personal computers (PC's), 67, 71
personal touch, 17
placement of ads, 109, 111
planning, 113–121
   checklist, 119–121
   elements, 114–118
   mailing lists, 46, 51
   overview and importance, 16,
      113–114, 139–140, 144, 147
postcards, 21, 80–82, 84–87, 93–95
Post-it Notes, 147
Potentials in Marketing, 32
premiums, 32
Premiums Magazine, 32
"price of admission," 29, 79
privacy policies, 61
prospects, 12–13, 23–24, 41–42, 44–45,
   51, 79–80
Prudential Douglas Elliman, 78, 137–139
public speaking, 150
publications, real estate, 54–55, 105

questionnaires, 21, 22, 45, 51, 73,
   89–90, 150

radio, 14, 110
rates, response. *See* responses
reach, 53–54, 63

real estate publications, 54–55, 105
Realtor Magazine, 54–55
Reeves, Rosser, 146
referrals, 33–34, 45, 83, 86
relationship building
  importance of, 1–7
  techniques, 57, 63–64, 89–90, 93,
     109, 151
  using direct marketing for, 17,
     21–22, 79–80, 102
ReMax, 45, 78, 137
rentals, list, 46–47, 160
responses, 13–14, 159. *See also* lead
    generation
  acting on, 74–75, 93
  tracking and evaluating, 3–4, 6,
     15–21, 35–38, 110–111, 126–132
results. *See* responses
retention programs, 33, 160
revenue, incremental, 123–126, 131
ROI (return on investment), 71
roll out, 128, 131, 161
Rubin, Denise, 137, 143
Ruff, Howard, xv

Salloom, Simon, 80–82
Schwartz, Barry, 150–151
scientific advertising, 146
search engines, 55
seasonality, 161
sectional centers (SCF's), 47, 161
security, online, 61
segmenting, 72–75
selections, list, 46–51
self-mailers, 93–95, 161
selling, 79–80, 145–147
seminars, 36, 149
Shopenn, Michael, 105–106
Silverman, Diane, 82–85
Smith, P.J. Martin, 139–140
software, 68–69
solo mailings, 86, 161
source codes, 19, 35, 111, 161
space ads, 14, 97–109, 151–154, 157,
    161–162
speaking, public, 150
spreadsheet software, 68

staff development, 143–144
status, lead, 75
strategies, 22, 79–80, 116, 120
strengths and weaknesses, 142–143
surveys, 21, 22, 45, 51, 73, 89–90, 150
sweepstakes, 34–35

tactics, 116–117, 120
target markets, 12–13, 23–24, 41–45, 51,
    79–80, 117
team work, 143–144
technology, xii, 143
television, 14, 110
testimonials, 12, 59, 100, 162
testing
  cells and tracking grids, 35–36,
     126–132, 162
  creative, 102–103
  offers, 18–21, 34–36
  overview, 3–4, 15–16
"thank you" gifts, 45, 87, 141–142, 144
Third Class mail, 162
3M, 147
Time, 124
timetables, 118, 121
tracking results, 6, 15–16, 18–21, 35–36,
    38, 110–111
"Tycoon, The," 147–148

understanding client needs, 134–135
URLs, 55

Village Voice, 103

Wall Street Journal, 97, 104
weaknesses and strengths, 142–143
web optimization, 54
websites, 53–62, 70–71, 150, 162
Weight Watchers, 116
Weithorn, Mark, 54–55, 58
"what's in it for me" (WII-FM), 11–13, 78
Wilf, Orin, 148
Word, Microsoft, 68
working from a knowledge level, 45

Zeckendorf Marketing, 61, 148–149
ZIP codes, 43, 47, 162